ON THE
JOB
SERIES

REAL PEOPLE WORKING *in*

COMMUNICATIONS

D1066691

ON THE
JOB
SERIES

REAL PEOPLE
WORKING *in*

COMMUNICATIONS

Jan Goldberg

Printed on recyclable paper

VGM Career Horizons
a division of *NTC Publishing Group*
Lincolnwood, Illinois USA

Library of Congress Cataloging-in-Publication Data

Goldberg, Jan
    Real people working in communications / Jan Goldberg.
        p.   cm. — (On the job)
    Includes bibliographical references.
    ISBN 0-8442-4730-8 (cloth)
    ISBN 0-8442-4731-6 (paper)
        1. Communications—Vocational guidance—United States.   2. Mass
media—Vocational guidance—United States.   I. Title.   II. Series.
    P91.6.G65   1996
    384′.023′73—dc20   96-28072
                                         CIP

Published by VGM Career Horizons
A division of NTC/Contemporary Publishing Group, Inc.
4255 West Touhy Avenue, Lincolnwood (Chicago), Illinois 60646-1975 U.S.A.
Copyright © 1997 by NTC/Contemporary Publishing Group, Inc.
All rights reserved. No part of this book may be reproduced, stored in a retrieval
system, or transmitted in any form or by any means, electronic, mechanical,
photocopying, recording, or otherwise, without the prior permission of
NTC/Contemporary Publishing Group, Inc.
Printed in the United States of America
International Standard Book Number: 0-8442-4730-8 (cloth)
                                      0-8442-4731-6 (paper)

20   19   18   17   16   15   14   13   12   11   10   9   8   7   6   5   4   3   2

Contents

Acknowledgments

The author gratefully acknowledges:

- The numerous professionals who graciously agreed to be profiled in this book.

- My dear husband Larry for his love, help, and support.

- My children, Deborah, Bruce and Sherri, for their encouragement and love.

- Family and close friends for their love and support: Adrienne, Marty, Mindi, Cary, Michele, Paul, Michele, Alison, Steven, Marci, Steven, Brian, Jesse, Bertha, Aunt Estelle, Uncle Bernard, Aunt Helen.

- Betsy Lancefield, editor at VGM, for making the project such a rewarding and enjoyable experience.

- Sarah Kennedy, former editor at VGM, for her guidance and vision.

- Diana Catlin, for her insights, input, and inspiration.

- My co-developer Blythe Camenson, for her hard work and sunny disposition.

This book is dedicated to the memory of my parents, Sam and Sylvia Lefkovitz.

About the Author

Jan Goldberg's love affair with the printed page began well before her second birthday. Regular visits to the book bindery where her grandfather worked produced a magic combination of sights and smells that she carries with her to this day.

Childhood was filled with composing poems and stories, reading books, and playing library. Elementary and high school included an assortment of contributions to school newspapers. While a full-time college student, Goldberg wrote extensively as part of her job responsibilities in the College of Business Administration at Roosevelt University in Chicago. After receiving a degree in elementary education, she was able to extend her love of reading and writing to her students.

Goldberg then began her career as a poet, and her work appeared in *Bell's Letters, Complete Woman*, and a number of poetry anthologies. She won several awards, including first place in a *Bell's Letters* contest. Her varied career also branched into book reviews for several periodicals, including *The Bloomsbury Review*.

As a business writer, Goldberg has been a regular contributor to The Dartnell Corporation for the past six years. She has authored pamphlets, bi-monthly articles, and quizzes for six sales instructional and motivational publications, and also writes for a management-level newsletter.

Goldberg has written extensively in the occupations area for General Learning Corporation's *Career World Magazine*, as well as for the many career publications produced by CASS Recruitment Publications. She has also contributed to a number of projects for educational publishers, including Scott Foresman and Addison-Wesley.

As a feature writer, Goldberg's work has appeared in *Today's Chicago Woman, Opportunity Magazine, Chicago Parent, Complete Woman, North Shore Magazine*, and Pioneer Press newspapers. In all, she has published more than 200 pieces as a freelance writer.

Goldberg is the author of *Careers in Journalism* and *Opportunities in Horticulture Careers*, both published in 1995 by VGM Career Horizons. She is the co-developer of the *On the Job* series.

How to Use This Book

On the Job: Real People Working in Communications is part of a series of books designed to serve as companion books to the *Occupational Outlook Handbook (OOH)*. The *OOH* is a useful reference book for librarians, guidance and career counselors, and job seekers. It provides information on hundreds of careers, focusing on the following subjects:

Nature of the work

Working conditions

Employment

Training, other qualifications, and advancement

Job outlook

Earnings

Related occupations

Sources of additional information

What the *OOH* doesn't provide is a first-hand look at what any particular job is *really* like. That's where the *On the Job* series picks up the slack. In addition to providing an overview of each field and a discussion of the training and education requirements, salary expectations, related fields, and sources to pursue for further information, *On the Job* authors have interviewed dozens of professionals and experts in the various fields.

These first-hand accounts describe what each job truly entails, what the duties are, what the lifestyle is like, and what the upsides and downsides are. The professionals we've spoken with reveal why they were drawn to the field and how they got started in it. And in order to help you make the best career choice for yourself, each professional offers you some expert advice based on years of personal experience.

Each chapter also lets you see at a glance, with easy to reference symbols, the level of education and salary range required for the featured occupations.

So, how do you use this book? It's easy. You don't need to run to the library or buy a copy of the *OOH*. All you need to do is glance through our extensive table of contents, find the fields that interest you, and read what the experts have to say.

Introduction to the Field

In today's world there is a heavy focus on communications. Truly, we are an information society. As E.B. White said many years ago, "All writing is communication; creative writing is communication through revelation–it is the self escaping into the open. No writer long remains incognito."

Creative writing is just one area in this vast industry. Communications is a large field that encompasses many different types of careers, as you can no doubt see by glancing at the table of contents of this book.

All the careers outlined in this book have some factors in common, but they are nevertheless distinctly different. Read through the chapters to hone in on the differences, and pay special attention to the interviews of individuals who are working in the field. They will provide you with special insights about the day-to-day life of performing that job. As you are perusing the book, ask yourself the following questions:

- How much time and money am I willing to devote to preparing myself for this career? Some careers require more education and training than others.

- Am I willing to "work my way up" from an entry level beginning?

- Do I enjoy working with people? Or am I happier working on my own?

- What are my salary goals? There are distinct differences between various careers.

- Do I enjoy work that puts me "on the edge," or am I more comfortable in a "safe" environment?

- Am I satisfied performing work that is repetitive or do I become bored easily?

- Do I want the assurances given to a full-time hired employee or am I more excited at the prospect of being self-employed?

- How well do I work under stress? Am I able to deal well with deadlines?

- Do I want a nine-to-five job or am I willing to work longer hours?

- Am I willing to relocate in order to advance my career?

This book will provide valuable information on working conditions and lifestyles so that you can make good choices based upon reliable facts.

Although *On the Job: Real People Working in Communications* strives to be as comprehensive as possible, not all jobs in this enormous field have been covered or given the same amount of emphasis. If you still have questions after reading this book, there are a number of other avenues to pursue. You can find more information by contacting the sources listed at the end of each chapter. You can also locate professionals on your own to talk to and observe as they go about their work. Any remaining gaps in your understanding of a particular occupation can be filled by referring to the *Occupational Outlook Handbook*.

1

Newspaper Publishing

OVERVIEW

"Journalists are people who peek through keyholes, wake people up in the middle of the night, and steal pictures from old ladies," says Pat O'Brien as the main character in the 1931 Howard Hughes film classic *The Front Page*. The movie, written by the journalist, author, and screenwriter Ben Hecht, along with Charles MacArthur, presents the story of an escaped prisoner who is sentenced to hang for the murder of a policeman. At the core of the movie is a press room and a handful of card-playing, smoking, biased, ill-mannered, and ill-tempered reporters. Hecht's own background as a *Chicago Daily News* staff writer and MacArthur's experiences as a *Hearst International Magazine* staff writer provide the background for this satirical and irreverent look at the conduct and character of reporters. Though few real reporters would actually want to resemble the people portrayed in *The Front Page*, one theme is on-target. Newspaper publishing, to a great degree, still relies on the skills and essential qualities of its reporters.

EDUCATION
B.A./B.S. Required

$$$ SALARY/EARNINGS
$20,000 to $30,000

Reporters and Correspondents

Reporters have always played an important role in society and they continue to do so. They inform, educate, and entertain the public by preparing stories on local, regional, national, and international levels. Their articles are based upon research: the notes, taped interviews, or pictures that the reporter has taken at the scene of the incident; research gathered at libraries, public offices, businesses, agencies; and information gathered by intelligent and persistent use of the telephone. Information may be obtained through interviews, news conferences, printed reports, letters, news briefings and anywhere else a reporter's "nose for news" takes him or her. After researching a story, reporters organize their material, define their focus or slant, then write and rewrite the story as many times as necessary. Drawing on their analytical skills and an unbiased perspective, they strive to ascertain the who, what, where, why, when, and how of each incident.

General assignment reporters cover all kinds of stories–anything from a new grocery store opening to a murder for hire. Other reporters may be assigned to specific geographic areas ("beats") or certain topical beats, such as business, fashion, education, politics, or entertainment. This division of labor can make it advantageous to have a specialized areas of expertise. Beat reporters usually generate stories on their own, while general assignment reporters often find themselves working on stories that emanate from tips, press releases, wire service stories, or staff editors. National and foreign correspondents are stationed in large U.S. and foreign cities to report on current events.

Reporters on smaller publications may be expected to perform a wide range of roles, from covering all aspects of the news to taking photographs, writing headlines, laying out pages, editing wire service copy, and composing editorials. They might also sell subscriptions, solicit advertisements and perform general office work.

Since news can happen at any time and may include an element of danger, reporting can be a consuming career choice. Generally, reporters on morning papers work from late afternoon until midnight; those on afternoon or evening papers work from early morning until early or midafternoon. There is also the additional pressure of deadlines. But there *are* rewards, one of which is to see one of your stories in print, especially with your name (a byline) attached to it.

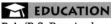 **EDUCATION**

B.A./B.S. Required

\$\$\$ SALARY/EARNINGS

$20,000 to $30,000

Investigative Journalists

While it is true that investigative journalists are reporters, there is an important distinction. These professionals don't simply report the news, they are often the ones to uncover newsworthy topics. It can take reporters days, weeks, or months while they delve into a particular story, putting the pieces of the puzzle together a little at a time. To accomplish this, investigative journalists must be creative, logical, and persistent. Additionally, they must have excellent interviewing skills in order to put people at ease so that they can elicit the information they are seeking.

EDUCATION

B.A./B.S. Required

\$\$\$ SALARY/EARNINGS

$20,000 to $30,000

Columnists

Although columnists must produce a specified number of articles each week, they have a decided luxury that most other newspaper writers don't have. They are allowed to choose their *own* topics and express their *own* viewpoints. As a result, their columns are usually a mixture of fact, opinion, and interpretative dialogue.

These regularly appearing articles are usually placed in the opinion or editorial section or in a special place in the newspaper so that readers know where to find them.

Columnists on large newspapers often become syndicated by selling their columns to other newspapers. There are literally hundreds of such columns available for purchase by publishers. *The Guinness Book of World Records* gives Ann Landers, whose column appears in over 1,200 newspapers, the distinction of being the most syndicated columnist.

EDUCATION

B.A./B.S. Required

\$\$\$ SALARY/EARNINGS

$20,000 to $30,000

Editorial Writers and Cartoonists

Editorial writers write opinion pieces designed to stimulate or mold public opinion in accordance with their newspaper's viewpoint. This is acceptable—that is, it does not violate the concept of an impartial press—because readers know that articles on editorial pages are opinions. Editorial cartoonists produce similar products, but use their artistic talents to express humor and often satire on education, politics, and societal issues or problems.

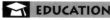

EDUCATION
B.A./B.S. Required

SALARY/EARNINGS
$20,000 to $30,000

Photojournalists

Photojournalists are reporters who have the ability to take pictures that tell the stories. They photograph newsworthy events, people, and places for publication in newspapers, magazines, and journals. Talented photojournalists recognize that it is the human element–namely, the relationship between individuals and events–that is important to highlight in their work, not necessarily the event itself.

For over a hundred years, newspapers have been publishing photographs. Until only a few decades ago, however, photojournalists were simply people with cameras who placed themselves in the middle of a catastrophe and were ready to take pictures. Today's photojournalist is more likely to be a college graduate, often with a degree in journalism or a related field. He or she must possess the artistic talent necessary to implement harmony, visual attractiveness, and proper balance. In addition to these skills, the photojournalist must be proficient in using camera equipment effectively.

Varied talents, such as being capable of writing copy to accompany photos, will increase opportunities for promotion. Photojournalists may become picture editors, chief photographers, or graphics directors.

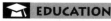

EDUCATION
B.A./B.S. Required

SALARY/EARNINGS
$20,000 to $30,000

Editors

Editors are a vital component of every news operation and serve as the coordinators of all newsgathering activities. Their primary duties include planning the contents of the newspapers and supervising their preparation. Working with reporters, photographers, and freelance and staff writers, editors are responsible for choosing, assigning, and overseeing copy to make sure that it meets the proper specifications for publication. Pieces must be checked for accuracy, grammar, spelling, and overall writing quality. Stories cannot contain any false statements and must be in line with the newspaper's overall style. Headlines may need to be written, and some editors have responsibilities in the layout of the publication. As editorial decisions are made, stories may be rewritten, trimmed, or lengthened, and pictures are selected. Sometimes the copy may be returned to reporters or writers for further attention, or may be rewritten by the editor. Combining reporters' articles, wire service stories, and syndicated columns, editors organize and prepare the final product.

The specific duties, number, and titles of editors vary according to the size of the newspaper. The managing editor or editor-in-chief is usually at the top of the editorial hierarchy; he or she is the one who oversees the day-to-day operation, guiding the newspaper in the direction the editor envisions for it. Often the editor writes the editorials that set the tone and style of the paper. Additionally, the editor may preside over editorial meetings and select personnel, including staff writers, freelance writers, reporters, editors, and other employees.

The editor in charge of assigning stories to reporters may be the city editor, news editor, or managing editor. On larger papers an executive editor oversees associate or assistant editors, who have responsibility for particular subjects, such as fiction, local news, international news, or sports, or who edit one or more special publications.

On smaller newspapers, editors perform a great variety of tasks. They may be responsible for reporting, writing, editing, taking photographs, and planning budgets. They may also handle marketing, advertising, production, and circulation.

Because the job of the editor is so central to the process of putting out a newspaper, late-breaking news may translate into long hours.

 **EDUCATION**
B.A./B.S. Recommended

$$$ SALARY/EARNINGS
$20,000 to $30,000

Copy Editors

Assisting editors are entry-level employees who may have the title of copy editors, assistant editors, production assistants, or editorial assistants. As experts in punctuation, spelling, and grammar, they review text for mistakes in these areas. They are also responsible for checking manuscripts for readability, clarity, style, and agreement with editorial policy. Editorial assistants may also perform research by verifying facts, dates, and statistics, or arrange page layouts of articles, photographs, and advertising. Copy editors may be involved in composing headlines, preparing copy for printing, and proofreading printer's galleys. Assistants on small papers often answer phones, make photocopies, and clip stories that come over the wire services' printers.

Deadlines are always looming, so these tasks need to be performed quickly and accurately.

Most copy editors work regular hours, totaling some 35 to 40 hours a week. However, others are called to work on weekends or at night to accommodate certain publications.

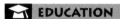
EDUCATION
B.A./B.S. Recommended

$$$ SALARY/EARNINGS
$12,000 to $20,000

Proofreaders

Proofreaders compare typeset material with original manuscripts to uncover any discrepancies in copy or composition. They search for mistakes in spelling or punctuation, missing text, wrong page numbers, typographical errors, or incorrect typefaces. They make sure that pictures are in the proper place and are the proper size. When mistakes are found, they mark them with proofreaders' symbols, which instruct the typesetter where to make the corrections.

Working a 35- to 40-hour week in this job is quite demanding, as the position requires long periods of close concentration.

TRAINING FOR NEWSPAPER PUBLISHING PERSONNEL

In days of yore, young adults who had a desire to enter the world of journalism could complete high school, present themselves at a local newspaper, and work their way up the ranks in the industry. This is no longer the case. Today's employers seek individuals with college degrees and experience. Some prefer liberal arts degrees; others prefer journalism, English, or communications degrees.

Over 300 colleges offer bachelor's degree programs in journalism. About 75 percent of these journalism programs focus on liberal arts courses, while the remaining 25 percent of a student's time is spent in journalism classes. Community and junior colleges also offer journalism classes (or programs) and these are often accepted for credit at four-year institutions. Master's degree programs are offered by approximately 100 schools; several offer PhDs in journalism.

Obviously, it is important for individuals in newspaper publishing to have considerable writing expertise and a love for this type of work. Word processing and desktop publishing skills are also an asset, as well as a wide ranging background and specific training in business, speech, foreign language, and computer science. Other desirable personal qualities include a "nose for news," curiosity, good judgment, creativity, self-motivation, veracity, persistence, a good memory, "people skills," ability to deal with pressure, and physical and emotional stability.

Those new to the field should expect to work their way "up the ladder," starting on smaller daily, weekly, local, suburban, or trade newspapers or perhaps as "stringers" (part-time employees who are paid by the story). Once they have gained valuable experience, individuals may then be considered for employment at larger publications or on newspapers in bigger cities.

JOB OUTLOOK

Because so many people are attracted to the newspaper publishing field, competition for jobs is very keen. In spite of this, the following job outlook through the year 2005 is expected:

Reporters and correspondents–as fast as average

Photojournalists–as fast as average

Writers and editors–as fast as average

Copy editors and proofreaders–little change expected

SALARIES FOR NEWSPAPER PERSONNEL

The Newspaper Guild negotiates with individual newspapers on minimum salaries for both starting reporters and those still on the job after three to six years. This organization reports that the median minimum salary for reporters is around $406 a week. The median minimum weekly salary for reporters after three to six years on the job is around $654 a week.

According to a recent survey by the Dow Jones Newspaper Fund, starting salaries for editorial assistants and writers averages $20,000 annually. Those who had at least five years experience earned an average of more than $30,000 a year; senior editors at the largest newspapers earned over $60,000 a year.

The median annual earnings for salaried photographers is around $21,000. Photographers in the federal government average $33,000 a year.

RELATED FIELDS

In order to succeed in this profession, reporters and correspondents must write effectively and clearly. Writing ability is also essential for technical writers, advertising copy writers, public relations workers, educational writers, fiction writers, staff writers, biographers, freelance writers, and screenwriters. Additional communicators include radio and television announcers and teachers. Other jobs that require the visual arts talent necessary for photojournalists include illustrators, designers, painters, and sculptors.

INTERVIEW
Carole Goddard
Journalist, Editor, and Bureau Chief

Carole Goddard is a journalist, editor, and bureau chief for the Bannockburn Group of Pioneer Press Newspapers, which includes 11 newspapers.

What the Job's Really Like

"I am responsible for the news, features, photography, and sports coverage for 11 newspapers. Six editors report directly to me. I direct some projects, attend numerous meetings, write many reports, and try to ensure that every member of the Bannockburn editorial staff is working up to his or her potential. Doing that is hard to quantify, but our group wins its share of company and national newspaper awards, so it must be working.

"The best part of working in this field is the unpredictability. News is never the same in one week or one community. There's an incredible feeling of accomplishment when a complicated report all comes together and our readers are better informed for having read it. We all still get a wonderful rush when the paper is delivered and we can point to it and say, 'I did that.' Actually that was one of the hardest transitions for me– when I went from being a managing editor with responsibilities for a paper that I could point to each week as mine, and when I became an editor who was charged with the less-quantifiable job of adding depth to the paper.

"The worst part of this job is when you run out of time. We are always pushing the clock, trying to get one more interview, one more quote, one more fact that will really make the story come alive. Another 'worst' is seeing a mistake in the paper, from a misspelling to an error to a missing page."

How Carole Goddard Got Started

"A family member who happened to be a sports writer got me started in this business. About the time Title IX was passed, schools were scrambling to organize sports for their females. I ended up being 'volunteered' for the girls' sports beat at our local newspaper. I was stunned, but I had an English degree and, being an avid sports fan and voracious newspaper reader, I thought it might be fun.

"I'll never forget my first story. The family member who could have helped me was out of town, so I had to do the reporting and writing on my own. I carefully crafted my words and peppered the stories with what I was sure were brilliant quotes. When he returned, I couldn't wait to show him what talent he had unwittingly tapped. I'll never forget what happened. He read the stories quietly for a long time without saying a word. Then he said, 'Well, I think we can work together on this.'

"I was crushed. But, of course, I quickly realized that there was a lot more to newspaper reporting and writing than I had ever realized. After that, I took several journalism courses and read a number of good newspaper writers–a good way to learn about quality writing. And I was edited heavily and fully by my family member. I always encouraged him to be really tough on me, because that was the most effective teacher for me. Of course, that meant rewriting, rewriting, and more rewriting! I see quite a bit of sloppy writing and editing today, and it bothers me that our standards have relaxed so much.

"After that I volunteered to take on other assignments. Both my children were in school then, so I asked for the education beat. I asked a lot of questions in the beginning, but once I understood how the system worked, it was easy to make the intricacies of the school board meaningful for my readers. By the way, this should be a cardinal rule for every journalist. You can't really write about something if you don't understand what you're talking about.

"My school beat coverage made me realize that I truly liked newspaper reporting, and I asked to be considered for a full-time position if one should ever open up there. It did, and I was hired. Within three years, I was named managing editor. A few years later I was recruited by Pioneer Press and assumed the managing editor position in Oak Park, one of the company's most important communities. Going from a small, family-run operation to a large corporation was quite a shock, but I learned a great deal in the first few years thanks to a terrific editor who demanded excellence. Four years later, I was promoted to editor of one of the company's five bureaus (at the time). Since then I have worked as the editor for two other bureaus before assuming my present position as bureau chief."

Expert Advice

"My recommendation would be to become a specialist. Also, be sure you have a good fix on what it is you want to do.

"Reporters have to master a great deal of knowledge. And as the world becomes more complicated, many staff writers are focusing their energies on specific areas: the environment, courts, schools, taxation, business, and so on. They start as generalists, but work into a specialist slot. I would encourage anyone starting out to get a journalism degree and also focus on a strong minor to nail down some type of specialty. Another possibility is to channel your energies into an area once you get a job.

"Anyone interested in journalism should spend time figuring out what he or she wants to be: a top editor or a top reporter. Too many really first-class reporters are lured into becoming editors when what they really excel at is the reporting and writing. So they're promoted and they're miserable. Part of the learning process for each new newspaper employee ought to include time spent figuring out what area of the newspaper most appeals to him or her. If it's the editorial end, which facet–managing, editing, or reporting? Once you know this, you can direct your work into the area best suited for you."

INTERVIEW

Fredric N. Tulsky
Investigative Reporter

Fredric N. Tulsky has worked both as an investigative reporter and an investigative editor and is the recipient of many awards, most notably a Pulitzer Prize for investigative reporting in 1987. Other distinctions include a National Headliners Award for public service in 1987; a bronze medallion, SKX-SPJ for general reporting in 1977; the Heywood Broun Award, writing on behalf of the underprivileged in 1977; the grand prize, Robert F. Kennedy Journalism Award, writing on behalf of the disadvantaged in 1978; and the Gavel Award from the American Bar Association in 1978 and 1988. To add to his expertise, Tulsky earned a law degree from Temple University School of Law in 1984 and was awarded a Nieman fellowship at Harvard University for 1988–1989.

What the Job's Really Like

"To me, what makes journalism exciting is uncovering information that no one else has found. I take great pride in reporting; democracy means nothing if people are not informed.

"I guess I see investigative reporting as doing just that–uncovering information about people and institutions of power that had been unknown (often because someone has been hiding the information).

"Over the years, I have worked on many investigative projects, often alone and many times with at least one partner. The advantage of working with someone is that, on a long project, it is great to have someone to discuss the project with, to keep your sanity. Such projects often take anywhere from a few weeks to many months. The formula is usually the same–having an idea and using public records and people to document the idea.

"For me, what differentiates a good story from a great story is showing a pattern–for instance, one of abuse. If a policeman beats someone, that is a good newspaper story. But if the reporter checks the internal affairs records, court records, and other available sources and finds that the policeman has beaten five people over the years, then a good story becomes a great story.

"One example is a story I did in Philadelphia about defense attorneys who had made a practice of testifying, after their clients were convicted, that the client deserved a new trial because they themselves had performed so poorly. The first time I saw it happen, I was shocked. I was sitting in a small courtroom in a remote part of City Hall when the testimony occurred. I was there just to watch what happened, on the theory that the most likely place a reporter can find news is the place where no reporters go. After hearing this attorney testify about his failures, I was determined to find out if this was some fluke or part of a larger pattern. I spent weeks talking to other attorneys to see if they had seen anything like it. Slowly, but surely, I found one case here and one there. (Unlike most stories, there was no place to go look up 'times attorneys testified that they committed gross errors.') I then spent months documenting the anecdotes through court records and interviews.

"The best part of the work comes in that moment when you discover that you have found something newsworthy that has not come to the public's attention beforehand.

"Another one of the great things about the work is that it's always different. As a reporter, I would spend most of my time either on the telephone or out of the office, talking to people and going through records. I would either be pursuing a particular story or checking in with my steady diet of sources to see what new issues there were for me.

"The worst part is the weeks it takes chasing dead ends and slogging through records to get to that point. Equally bad is going to talk to someone whom you know will be the subject of negative publicity, and making sure that you have given him or her a full opportunity to tell his or her side."

How Fredric N. Tulsky Got Started

"For as long as I can remember I wanted to be a newspaper reporter. I grew up on newspapers. As a boy, I can remember the excitement of running outside early each morning to gather the morning papers and check the sports scores; and then again to read the afternoon paper each day after school.

"By high school, I became managing editor of the newspaper and subsequently attended college at the University of Missouri School of Journalism.

"For the grand sum of $120 per week, I landed my first job as an intern for the Saginaw, Michigan, *News*. After graduation, I returned to the paper as city hall reporter, and then went where the opportunities were: to Port Huron, Michigan; Jackson, Mississippi; Los Angeles, and then to the *Philadelphia Inquirer*, where I spent 14 years."

Expert Advice

"I think the ingredients for an investigative reporter are simple–persistence, passion, and care. You have to be willing to spend weeks going through records, prepared to find nothing. In looking for documentation, there is no need to behave badly. In fact, I believe people are more willing to help someone who is respectful, and I've adhered to that belief throughout my entire career."

INTERVIEW

Judy Markey
Columnist and Radio Personality

Judy Markey has been "chronicling the insanities, inequities, and the ironies of contemporary life" in her nationally syndicated thrice-week-

ly humor <u>Chicago Sun-Times</u> column for the past 10 years. Five years ago, WGN-Radio teamed Markey with Kathy O'Malley, a <u>Chicago Tribune</u> reporter. Together they host a daily afternoon talk show. She has appeared on "Today," "Oprah," Donahue," "Good Morning America," and "CBS This Morning."

Her first collection of essays, <u>How to Survive Your High School Reunion and Other Mid-Life Crises</u>, was published in 1984. Her subsequent collection, <u>You Only Get Married for the First Time Once</u>, was published in 1988.

What the Job's Really Like

"Every day means waking up and being nervous because I already know there are not enough hours in the day. Nevertheless, I try to write in the morning at home and gather a lot of articles that will either relate to the writing or the radio program, which are really intermingled. Then I like to get on my exercise machine and watch some morning shows, listen to the radio, and read two newspapers before the phones begin to ring at 9.

"I get to the radio station about 11:45 A.M. and sit down with some wire copy and a couple of papers that I don't get at home. After I do the show I go home and get back to the writing I started in the morning.

"I have to produce about 2100 words a week, three ostensibly cohesive ideas every week of my own invention. There are weeks when I sort of know what I'm going to write about. And I've done this for so long that even during those weeks when I'm not crazy about my ideas and it's already Wednesday, I don't panic because I always know I'll come up with something.

"Unless I plan a vacation, I have a seven-day work week. I love both of the things that I do, though, and realized that it was going to be like this. However, I don't think I would want to keep this up forever. Writing is gratifying, writing is joyful, but it's also just plain hard, hard work."

How Judy Markey Got Started

"Even though I graduated from Northwestern University's Medill School of Journalism, I was a late bloomer. I didn't start writing until I was 36. I began late because I wasn't ready to deal with the competition or the rejections that are common to a writing career. But by the time I reached this age, competition and rejection were no longer big issues.

"I began in my dining room on a typewriter, after first securing a large supply of envelopes (because I knew that things would be rejected). My first piece was sold to the *Chicago Tribune*, however, and I was really lucky because within a year I was published in five national magazines.

"The column came about in kind of a funny way. I didn't do article assignments for the *Sun Times* and work up to a column. I simply went in there and said I'd like to be a columnist. They kind of laughed and said, 'You just can't walk in here like this,' and I said, 'Oh!' Nevertheless they asked me to write some stories for them. Though I had a wonderful time writing the four stories we agreed upon, I was really not interested in writing newspaper articles because the pay isn't very good. This may sound avaricious but it also ties into pride about your work. Luckily for me, the *Sun Times* was great and offered me a once a week column, which became twice a week and then three times a week and then became syndicated.

"I've been really, really blessed because–though there was a lot of risk-taking in my career–there was a lot of serendipity involved. I didn't engineer things–they just sort of happened. I was well aware that I wasn't waking up in the morning salivating to go cover a city council meeting. It was clear that there was a certain kind of writing that I liked. But it's not for everyone. There are wonderful reporters at the paper who would no more want to do what I do than they would want to swim the English Channel. It seems too risky or too personal or too self indulgent. It wouldn't suit them. But it's perfect for me.

"From my vantage point, the best part of all of this is the constant learning and the free pass that I have, which allows me to enter people's lives. I don't say that with prurient interest. I just feel that I really learn a lot about humanity, because between a phone and a computer and the radio, people populate your lives in a very intense and personal way. Of course, seeing my byline is nice–that charges anyone up–but at this point I really love the fact that I virtually always have something interesting or funny that has crossed my path that day to pass along at the dinner table. I find it amazing. Conversely, the worst part is that I sometimes have the feeling that I have to be predatory, that I'm sometimes documenting life more than living it."

Expert Advice

"I certainly don't think it's necessary to get a master's degree in Communications, but I do think it's necessary to be genuinely curious about the world. The main thing you need to enable you to be really successful at anything is the ability to be resourceful. If you can't figure out how to get the answer to a question or where to go next, then you must be completely unafraid about asking. You must never be ashamed that you don't know something, because it isn't shameful to not know everything. It is just shameful not to be able to figure out how to obtain the information.

"It's also important to learn to think critically and be neither mentally or physically lazy. Never look for the easy way out. There are so many good people out there vying for the same slots that it's important to approach each situation honorably."

INTERVIEW
David Klobucar
Photojournalist

David Klobucar is a photojournalist employed by a large city newspaper, the Chicago Tribune.

What the Job's Really Like

"A typical week in the life of a photojournalist is probably a lot less exciting than people think. The day is broken into shifts from 7 A.M. until 11 or 12 at night with photojournalists putting in 8 hour shifts. About 30 to 45 minutes before my shift is supposed to start, I call in and find out if they have anything special for me to do. If they don't have any specific assignments for me that day, they tell me what general area of the city they want me in and I start driving into that area. If two photojournalists are assigned to one area, we head in opposite directions so that we have the area fully covered. I have two scanners in my car and a company radio, so if my office needs to get a hold of me they can contact me at any time with an assignment. Or if I hear something on the scanner that I think might be interesting I might check into it.

"We split the day between taking photographs and getting them ready for publication. If I were working a shift that started at 9 A.M., for example, I would stay out in the field until 2 or 3 P.M., then come back to the office to process what I'd done that day. (Most of the places I've worked at require you to develop your own film, but the big newspapers often have lab people who develop it for you.) After I edit my film, I decide which frames I want used and submit them to the picture editor. Since we don't make prints anymore–everything is electronic–I scan the image into a computer, attach that image to a caption and a slot that tells which story it goes with.

"If I come across any good stories that interest me, I can develop my own projects. For instance, a reporter and I were out at the Chicago Housing Authority one day talking with some security people. It occurred to me that these guards could form the basis of a great story profiling a new program recently launched there. The reporter and I subsequently 'pitched' the idea by making a proposal and turning it into our editor. If it's decided that the story is worthwhile, the reporter and I will combine our efforts. I prefer to work this way, because the images and the words tend to match a lot better if you're both seeing the same thing. If you don't work as a team, you're not telling the same story."

How David Klobucar Got Started

"I grew up in Kansas City and I attended Oak Park High School. In my junior year, I took a camera course and found I was really interested in photography. Then I signed up for the yearbook course and became the photographer for the yearbook, which developed my interests even further. After graduation I attended the University of Missouri at Columbia as a biochemistry major, but after a year I knew that I was going to have problems with classes like calculus. Discovering that the university had an excellent journalism program, I switched to my second love and earned a bachelor's degree in Journalism with a major in photography.

"For the next 10 years I accepted positions in Jackson, Mississippi; Omaha, Nebraska; and Springfield, Illinois. I was doing freelance work and somewhat disillusioned with the newspaper industry when my wife was offered a good position in Chicago and we moved there. After about six months, I received a call from the *Chicago Tribune* asking me to work part-time. I worked part-time for a year and a half until they asked me to become a full-time employee. It's funny—when I left Springfield I had no intention of going back into newspaper work, but I realized that though there were some things I didn't like about it, there were more that I did."

Expert Advice

"In order to be a successful photojournalist you must be a self-starter. If you don't take the initiative to seek out stories and show an interest in the world around you and how it all fits together, you will not succeed. You need to have curiosity about the world, about people, and about photojournalism. With the vision of a psychologist, you must be able to read people in order to help them understand what you're trying to do. A lot of people are very suspicious of what you are doing, but really you're simply trying to understand their world.

"You always need to remember that you are trying to be a visual communicator. The images need to be thoughtful and compelling in terms of composition, movement, and lighting. It's not just walking into a situation, clicking the shutter, and walking away.

"A lot of people think photojournalism is really easy and fun. Admittedly, it's a very interesting career, but it's also very demanding. There are a number of skills that you must bring to the job in order to produce exciting images. You don't use one skill at a time; you must have a bagful of skills at your disposal at all times."

●   ●   ●

See Chaper 3 for a profile of a book copyeditor.

FOR MORE INFORMATION

Additional information including pamphlets and brochures is available by contacting the following organizations:

Newspaper Association of America
The Newspaper Center
Box 17407
Dulles International Airport
Washington, DC 20041

Newspaper Association of America Foundation
11600 Sunrise Valley Drive
Reston, VA 22091

The Dow Jones Newspaper Fund, Inc.
P.O. Box 300
Princeton, NJ 08543–0300

The Newspaper Guild, Research and Information Department
8611 Second Avenue
Silver Spring, MD 20910

National Newspaper Association
1627 K Street N.W., Suite 400
Washington, DC 20006

Professional Photographers of America, Inc.
1090 Executive Way
Des Plaines, IL 60018

For a list of junior and community colleges offering journalism programs, contact the Community College Journalism Association, San Antonio College, 1300 San Pedro Avenue, San Antonio, TX 78212-4299.

For a list of schools whose journalism programs have been accredited, send a stamped, self-addressed envelope to Accrediting Council on Education in Journalism and Mass Communications, University of Kansas School of Journalism, Stauffer, Flint Hall, Lawrence, KS 66045.

For general information about careers in journalism, contact the Association for Education in Journalism and Mass Communication, University of South Carolina, 1621 College Street, Columbia, SC 29208-0251.

The following books are additional sources:

Goldberg, Jan. *Careers in Journalism.* Lincolnwood, Ill: NTC Publishing Group, 1995.

Harrigan, Jane T. *Read All About It! A Day in the Life of a Metropolitan Newspaper.* Chester, Conn: The Globe Pequot Press, 1988.

Noronha, Shonan, F. R. *Careers in Communications.* Lincolnwood, Ill: NTC Publishing Group, 1993.

Tebbel, John. *Opportunities in Newspaper Publishing Careers.* Lincolnwood, Ill: NTC Publishing Group, 1989.

Lists of schools, departments of journalism, and names and location of newspapers are published in the *Editor and Publisher International Year Book*, which you can find in most public libraries or newspaper offices.

CHAPTER 2 Magazine Publishing

OVERVIEW

Most newsstands are filled with a wide array of magazines, but a much larger number–literally thousands–remain unseen by the general public because they are handled by subscription to the buyer's home. Anyone with an interest in virtually anything can find a magazine devoted to that subject and immerse themselves in their favorite topic whenever they wish to do so. And apparently they do–according to the American Society of Magazine Editors, the average adult purchases 36 magazines per year.

Magazines are usually classified into two main categories: consumer magazines (those designed for mass audiences) and magazines written for trade, technical, and professional audiences.

The following are examples of consumer magazines: *Volleyball Magazine, True Confessions, Cincinnati Magazine, Bird Watcher's Digest, Current Health I, Country Home and Gardens, Longevity, Soap Opera Digest, Kiplinger's Personal Finance, Twins, American Careers*, and *Army Magazine*.

The following are examples of trade magazines: *The Horn Book Magazine, Self-Employed America, Teaching K-8, Ohio Farmer, 9-1-1-Magazine, Writer's Digest, Pest Management, MD Magazine, Opera News, Photo Lab Management, The Pet Dealer*, and *Canadian Printer*.

THE WORLD OF MAGAZINE PUBLISHING

Magazines differ from one another in a number of ways, but they all have a few things in common. For instance, the word 'story' refers to both fiction and nonfiction articles. *Pictures* represent all visual representations. *Layouts* are diagrams of how all material will be placed on the magazine's page. And there is an expectation that all magazines will print their publications on a regular schedule, whether it be weekly, monthly, bimonthly, or yearly.

The Editorial Staff

Although newspaper editorial staffs vary from one publication to another, most organizations consist of some combination of the following: a publisher, an editor-in-chief, an executive editor, a managing editor, associate editors, assistant editors, staff writers, copy editors, editorial assistants, and proofreaders.

An employee's title at one magazine does not necessarily translate to the same position at another company. Usually, though, the following titles include the described duties:

EDUCATION
Post Graduate Recommended

$$$ SALARY/EARNINGS
$40,000 to $50,000

PUBLISHER/EDITOR-IN-CHIEF. The very top of the editorial hierarchy—the person who is responsible for all facets and aspects of the magazine's operation.

EDUCATION
Post Graduate Recommended

$$$ SALARY/EARNINGS
$30,000 to $40,000

EXECUTIVE EDITOR. Next in line in the editorial hierarchy. This is mainly an administrative position with responsibilities for the day-to-day operation of the company. This individual may also be the one to compose essays or other opinion pieces, provide scheduling for the magazine, manage the staff, and serve as liaison between editorial and advertising departments.

EDUCATION
Post Graduate Recommended

$$$ SALARY/EARNINGS
$30,000 to $40,000

MANAGING EDITOR. Oversees all articles from staff writers, editors, and freelancers, and possibly from the public relations division. The managing editor also handles his or her own projects, such as writing and editing.

EDUCATION
B.A./B.S. Required

$$$ SALARY/EARNINGS
$20,000 to $30,000

EDUCATION
B.A./B.S. Recommended

$$$ SALARY/EARNINGS
$20,000 to $30,000

EDUCATION
B.A./B.S. Recommended
$$$ SALARY/EARNINGS
$20,000 to $30,000

EDUCATION
B.A./B.S. Recommended
$$$ SALARY/EARNINGS
$12,000 to $20,000

ASSOCIATE OR ASSISTANT EDITORS. Oversee projects and discuss story ideas with writers, keeping abreast of new trends and ideas.

EDITORIAL ASSISTANTS. In these entry level positions, employees conduct research, perform office duties, and in some cases provide the first screening of manuscripts that are submitted by writers. On smaller magazines, duties will include rewriting, copy editing, and proofreading.

COPY EDITORS. Examine manuscripts for errors in grammar, spelling, context, punctuation, style, and accuracy of ideas.

PROOFREADERS. Scrutinize galleys and page proofs before they go to press to make sure they match the original manuscript.

Some magazines also make use of contributing editors who are not on staff. These individuals are often former staff editors, and may be asked to create story ideas and assign the pieces, or write the articles themselves.

Photojournalists are just as important a part of a magazine's staff as they are for a newspaper. Many photojournalists serve as staff employees; others are hired to work on a freelance basis.

Editors' Responsibilities

Regardless of title, most editors are involved in the following three endeavors:

1. Creating ideas and themes for upcoming issues of the magazine

2. Wading through the article ideas submitted by mail or phone and deciding which to proceed with and who will write them

3. Making sure all articles are properly edited and ready for publication. This may involve revising, verifying facts, molding the copy into the required length, composing titles and captions, and reviewing galleys and page proofs.

Editors work closely with art departments and supervise the visual aspects of all articles. In order to meet deadlines, overtime hours are often mandatory.

Some editors have expertise in a particular area, such as fashion, sports, business, politics, or education. Because of this, they may be assigned appropriate special projects that require extensive research and development.

Since it is vital that editors and other staff members meet to discuss upcoming issues, editorial meetings are an integral part of the magazine publications process. Much of the editorial planning is carried on months in advance in order to make all the necessary decisions, meet deadlines, and maintain a high level of journalism.

TRAINING FOR MAGAZINE PUBLISHING PERSONNEL

For those interested in entering the magazine publishing field, a degree in English, journalism, communications or, in some cases, liberal arts, is usually expected. Many colleges and universities offer coursework specifically in magazine writing, production, and aspects of publishing. These experiences are assets for beginners in this field.

A magazine internship can give you a solid 'foot in the door.' Combine your degree with job experience related to school, local, or other magazine publishing, and you have the makings of acceptance to an entry-level magazine position. Add to this a facility for generating story ideas and development; solid writing, copyediting, and proofreading abilities; and editing, research and interviewing skills–and your chances are excellent!

JOB OUTLOOK

According to the *Occupational Outlook Handbook*, careers in magazine publishing are expected to grow as fast as average. Competition will remain keen, with greater numbers of positions continuing to exist in San Francisco, Boston, Chicago, New York, Los Angeles, Washington, D.C., and Philadelphia.

SALARIES FOR MAGAZINE PUBLISHING PERSONNEL

Salaries in all positions vary considerably and depend on the size and location of the publication, in addition to the credentials and experience of the candidate. Starting salaries for writers and editorial assistants average about $20,000 per year; usually this is for a 35- to 40-hour week. After about five years, the salary rises to about $30,000. Writers and editors employed by the federal government average around $40,000. Associate editors average in the upper twenties; senior and managing editors in the mid- to upper-thirties range; and editors-in-chief in the lower-forties range.

RELATED FIELDS

All the careers discussed in this book are related to jobs in magazine publishing: newspaper publishing, book publishing, radio and television, advertising and public relations, other types of writing, and teaching. Every one of these careers focuses on the communication of ideas and information.

INTERVIEW
Timothy M. Clancy
Executive Editor

Timothy M. Clancy oversees the editorial production of 150 annual and bimonthly career development publications for college and university students and for minority professionals at CASS Recruitment

Publications. He is also responsible for the hands-on editing of approximately 50 college <u>Placement Manuals</u>, as well as for nine annual minority <u>Career Development Guides</u> and the EEO bimonthly magazine.

What the Job's Really Like

"Since my division is small in terms of number of employees, my responsibilities are varied. On any given day I may have to talk to many career services professionals at the colleges for which we publish career materials; edit an original article; work with the graphic designer on color selection for a brochure, magazine cover or article layout; discuss the wording of a promotional piece with a sales representative; review a pre-press blueline proof; help a job seeker locate career information (phone calls of this nature are directed to me); administer a proofreading test; and conduct job interviews.

"There's enough variety to keep it interesting. More important, though, is the rewarding nature of the job, since I am able to provide quality publications free of charge to many of the top schools in the country. Each *Placement Manual* is unique to its respective university and paid for by recruitment ads from companies that are seeking new grads. I get a lot of phone calls and letters from the career services directors at these schools telling me how much they appreciate what we are able to do for them. That feels really good, especially after working long hours during the main production cycle in the spring and summer.

"One down side to this kind of position is that there are times when the stress level is very high: I must juggle many projects at one time, deal with emotions that accompany a heavy workload, and watch a pile of paperwork grow to the size of a small city."

How Timothy M. Clancy Got Started

"My entry into journalism was more happenstance than calculation. I was not interested in journalism in high school, though my writing always earned high marks. I originally planned to pursue a degree in optometry or psychology. During the summer between my freshman and sophomore years in college, I noticed that most of my friends were on the school newspaper. I decided to take some journalism classes and see what attracted my friends. Before I knew it, I was news editor and the following semester, I was named executive editor! It seems that I had found my niche. Suddenly the calculus and pre-med classes weren't nearly as exciting as being a reporter.

"I realized that the chances of making much money as a reporter were rather slim, and being greedy and materialistic (remember, this was the 1980s!), I decided to pursue corporate employment. So I elected to take a public relations option within my journalism degree. I planned to get into some sort of corporate communications environment, as opposed to 'hard' journalism.

"Unfortunately, when I was in college, there were very few internships available for public relations students and fewer still on-campus interviews for journalism majors seeking professional employment. So while the high-tech firms were battling in the college placement office for engineers and computer scientists, we liberal arts types had a much harder time locating potential employers. Had I known then what I do now (as far as implementing your own job search plan), I probably would have secured a position faster. After sending out many rèsumès and cover letters, I received only one interview offer, for a management trainee position at a mid-level department store chain. I went to the interview and was so confident that I was going to get the job that I immediately rewarded myself by going on a little shopping spree. Well, I didn't get the job, but I had a nice suit to wear to subsequent interviews!

"Just when I thought my future had literally gone to the dogs (I was working in a pet store), I received a phone call from Career Research Systems, a company that I had applied to for a part-time proofreader position two years earlier. They had kept my rèsumè on file and called me back for an interview–this time for a permanent full-time editorial position. I got the job and now, 12 years (and several changes of ownership) later, I have risen up the ranks to my current position as executive editor."

Expert Advice

"I would tell those interested in a publishing career to keep abreast of the changing technology of electronic publishing.

Don't accept your first position with a company that does things 'the old way' with conventional typesetting and mechanical paste-up (amazingly there are still companies that are in the technological Dark Ages). Try to get enough knowledge of desktop publishing so that you can interface effectively with designers, art directors, and typographers. If there's a downside to the new technology, it's that some of the smaller companies are using their editors as designers, requiring them to do the actual layout and design, rather than hiring art directors. The net result is that there's a lot of amateurish and/or hackneyed desktop publishing happening. Find a company that is utilizing the new technology to its fullest–to enhance the final product, rather than using it to cut corners. It's good to get cross-trained in other areas, but in most cases, an editor/designer is probably neither a great editor nor a great designer. What I'm saying is: Develop your expertise in your career discipline and then enhance your marketability by developing a working knowledge of peripheral disciplines. In my case, it means focusing on editorial skills, but also understanding college/employer relations, typography and design, personnel matters, and the actual printing process."

INTERVIEW

Mary Haley
Managing Editor

Mary Haley is Managing Editor of <u>Chicago Parent News Magazine</u>, which was honored by Northwestern University's Medill School of Journalism with the General Excellence Award for 1992 and again in 1994. <u>Chicago Parent</u> was chosen as the top parenting publication from among parenting publications across the nation.

What the Job's Really Like

"It is the editor's responsibility to have a vision of where a publication is going and to provide it with a distinctive tone. The publishing cycle determines the day-to-day experiences of an editor. Since *Chicago Parent* is a monthly publication, I typically find myself spending two weeks on short- and long-range planning and two weeks on the editing and production cycle.

"Feature stories are planned out and assigned two to three months in advance. Most stories and regular features are assigned to freelance writers, but occasionally an unsolicited manuscript may be included (and all manuscripts must be read). We have a number of authors who write for us on a regular basis, but it is also important to continually find new voices for the publication. Photos and illustrations are usually assigned a month in advance of publication, as is the cover photo. Editing is done a week or more in advance of the production cycle. Headlines are written in collaboration with the page layout designer before pages are designed. On deadline day, all pages are reviewed as page assembly is completed. However, these days are numbered. Soon the magazine will be sent to the printer on disk.

"In addition, I develop a yearly editorial budget and provide the financial manager with monthly totals, as well as with information on payments to be made to writers, illustrators, and photographers.

"And, of course, there is the mail. Opening it can be both the most interesting and the most routine part of the day. But one thing is certain—we're never short on volume.

"For me, the best part about working for *Chicago Parent* is that it allows me to combine two great interests: children and editorial work. It's tremendously rewarding to think that we could have a positive impact on the quality of children's lives, while providing their parents with information, support, and encouragement.

"The worst part, I suppose, is the unrelenting nature of deadlines. But you have to learn early to live with them or you've chosen the wrong career."

How Mary Haley Got Started

"My work history falls into three fairly distinct parts, and forms, I like to think, some kind of a logical progression. I worked for 10 years as an elementary school teacher for the Archdiocese of Chicago, teaching fourth through eighth grades. After that, I accepted a position with Scott Foresman, a publisher of educational materials. At the time, the company was hiring a number of former teachers in the hopes that they could provide realistic information from the 'front lines' to use in the development of their various products.

"During my three years at Scott Foresman, I worked on a reading series for students with special needs. It was there that I had my first editing experience in an intensive, hands-on environment. We were responsible for everything from selecting and developing content material to tracking skills presentations, adjusting readability levels, assigning and reviewing freelance materials, and reviewing artwork. It was a trial-by-fire experience and a tremendous opportunity to learn first-hand what goes into taking a project from the idea stage to the presses.

"In 1980 my husband Dan put together a group of investors and launched *Wednesday Journal*, a locally owned community newspaper in Oak Park, Illinois. By 1984, the *Journal* was getting its feet on the ground, but the position of feature editor had turned over several times in less than a year. Dan was looking for someone who could bring stability to the position, and I suggested that I might be that person. We have been working together ever since. I worked as feature editor for the *Journal* for the next six years, developing story ideas and editing copy, working with freelance writers and photographers, and in the early years, designing my own pages.

"Wednesday Journal Inc. was looking for an expansion opportunity in 1990 when *Chicago Parent* became available. Following the purchase of *Chicago Parent*, I became editor.

"My educational background includes a B.A. in English, and I completed the coursework for a master's in English at the University of Minnesota. I learned by doing, perhaps not the easiest approach. But for me, being here is something that evolved rather than a goal that I set early for myself."

Expert Advice

"I think a degree in journalism can provide a valuable grounding and realistic preparation for someone entering the field. But beyond professional preparation I would look for a person who has a high energy level and is willing to commit to hard work, is attentive to detail and likes to delve into a topic or project, is widely read and fundamentally interested in the world around (him or) her, has a positive nature, and is able to work well with people."

INTERVIEW

Christen P. Heide
Executive Editor

Christen Heide is Executive Editor for *Sales and Marketing Publications* at The Dartnell Corporation. He is a respected speaker and writer of sales compensation and sales force management. His articles have appeared in such publications as <u>Advertising Age</u> and <u>Marketing News</u>, and he is widely quoted in the business press as a sales and marketing authority. He recently addressed the 54th International Marketing Congress of Sales and Marketing Executives International (SMEI) on contemporary issues in compensation and has been a featured sales compensation speaker at the Sales and Marketing Executives Society of Houston and Sales and Marketing Executives of Corpus Christi, Texas. Additionally, he appeared on INC. magazine's "Fourth Annual Growing The Company Conference" program, where he spoke on using sales incentives to boost sales performance.

What the Job's Really Like

"My main responsibility is to direct the editorial focus and content of the sales and marketing publications from conceptualization to final printed product. I function as editor and/or author for other printed material on an as-needed basis.

"My general editorial duties focus on generating appropriate articles for publication. This includes assigning articles to freelance writers, working with outside public relations firms, research companies, CEOs, presidents, sales managers, and the like to develop story ideas and produce finished stories.

"I edit, rewrite, or self-generate all materials for publication. This includes specifying type, writing headlines, selecting photos and/or graphics, writing captions, and general layout.

"Functioning as survey director and author for our Sales Force Compensation Survey, I work closely with the Sales and Marketing Executives International headquarters to produce an association newsletter.

"I am also responsible for training new editors and working with department heads on an as-needed, per-project basis; other duties include providing media interviews as necessary and maintaining ongoing press relations and author contacts.

"All days are similar in one respect—they are focused around producing publications on schedule. Activities that take you away from this are very much a part of the job and must be dealt with creatively. Deadline pressure is a constant; however, you have a great deal of freedom determining how to spend your time. The one catch is, when the time is up, you'd better be ready! Playing catch up is nerve-wracking and detracts from quality. So many things must get done at the same time.

"There is a wonderful sense of accomplishment when major projects are completed. Working in a creative field brings great satisfaction, because something brand new exists because of your efforts.

"Unlike other occupations, journalists can continue to work on a freelance basis after normal retirement. Carpenters, for instance, face the limitations of age and physical ability. But writing requires very little of a person physically. As long as you can think and hold a pencil, you can work almost anywhere. This type of career can give you untold amounts of freedom. However, any job can get tedious if you let it. But if you keep challenging yourself, the monotonous parts will be easier to take."

How Christen P. Heide Got Started

"I attended Lawrence University (Appleton, Wisconsin), the University of Pittsburgh (Pittsburgh, Pennsylvania), and the University of Wisconsin in Madison, Wisconsin, concentrating in philosophy and English and earning a double major. The two fields are an excellent combination; philosophy gives you the 'big picture' and teaches you how to think by giving you a good grounding in logic; English, literature, creative writing, and basic grammar give you the tools to put your thoughts on paper.

"Interestingly, back in the late 1960s and early 1970s, some employers viewed a journalism degree as a negative. In fact, the editorial department of one 80,000 circulation daily paper made a point of *not* hiring journalism graduates. You were hired on the basis of interest in the field and writing ability. (And if you had an insatiable desire to work terrible hours for low pay, the hiring decision was easier still!) In the beginning, you go where the work is; later you can be selective. For me, this meant positions at *Reader's Digest* in New York City, Ad/Mar Research in New York City, a variety of freelance jobs in New York; the *Milwaukee Star News*, a Milwaukee weekly, *The News-Gazette* and the *Journal Herald* in Winchester, Indiana; and the *Journal Gazette* in Fort Wayne, Indiana. The positions ranged from reporter to managing editor."

Expert Advice

"Anyone considering this field must like to read, like to be challenged, and like hard work. I would recommend that you learn all you can about word usage and grammar–and really know it well. Many people wash out because they don't have the basic foundation of skills. You've got to be detail-minded and take pride in a job well done. Mistakes are costly.

"What someone really needs is a love of language in order to appreciate its nuances, its richness, its variety, its playfulness. For the power of language lies in its ability to create new thoughts, inspire people to action, amuse and entertain, and pursue the truth."

• • •

FOR MORE INFORMATION

Contact the following organizations for additional information:

American Society of Magazine Editors
575 Lexington Avenue
New York, NY 10022

Magazine Publishers of America
575 Lexington Avenue
New York, NY 10022

Consult the following for additional information:

Pattis, S. William. *Opportunities in Magazine Publishing Careers.* Lincolnwood, Ill: NTC Publishing Group, 1992.

Fredette, Jean M. (Editor). *Handbook of Magazine Article Writing.* Cincinnati, Ohio: Writer's Digest Books, 1988.

Folio Magazine, Cowles Business Media, P.O. Box 4949, 911 Hope Street, Stamford CT 06907-0949. *Folio* is a monthly publication that focuses on the magazine industry.

CHAPTER 3 Book Publishing

OVERVIEW

The world of books is one of wonder and magic–it takes us to far away places to experience things we might never dream of or know about otherwise. Books are a living chronicle of generations past, contemporary times, and decades to come. In allowing us to escape from the stresses and strains of our everyday existences, books provide information, relaxation, elucidation, and inspiration. As John Milton once said, "A good book is the precious life-blood of a master spirit, embalmed and treasured up on purpose to a life beyond life."

Every book that is written begins as an idea, whether it comes from a prospective author or an editor. If it comes from an editor, then that individual will seek out an author he or she knows to have a solid record of writing performance.

If the idea stems from an author, he or she must compose an outline and at least several sample chapters so that the editor can judge whether both the idea and the would-be author are credible. (In some cases, publishers ask to see the entire book.) Some book publishers will only deal with an author's representative (agent); book proposals can only be presented to these publishers through agents.

Since publishers usually specialize in particular genres, the world of books is divided into several categories. These include trade book publishers, paperback publishers, textbook publishers, small press and university publishers, and religious presses.

Company size will determine the number of editors on staff at any publisher. The editorial hierarchy will vary from one publisher to another, but usually one editor stays involved in a book's progress from the inception of the idea to the finished product. In this regard, one editor is then responsible for negotiating with the author to establish advances, deadline dates, and royalty percentages–in addition to other terms, such as the expected form and content of the finished manuscript.

Most editors will be called upon to write book jacket copy, author biographies, press releases, and memos.

Trade Book Publishers

In the world of book publishing, the term "trade books" (also referred to as "mass market") includes books intended for the general population. This huge category includes both fiction and non-fiction genres, such as mysteries, romances, science fiction, historical fiction, and biographies.

Entering this field is usually accomplished by acquiring a lower-level position as an editorial assistant who is responsible for office duties (answering the phone, filing, making copies, handling correspondence) and screening manuscripts that are submitted to editors.

The next step up would be to the position of assistant editor. At this level, you can expect to read a lot of manuscripts, write book jacket copy, and provide whatever assistance is needed by your superiors.

Other positions available up the editorial ladder include junior editor, associate editor, acquisitions editor, editor, senior editor, and executive or managing editor. In most cases, a 35- to 40-hour week is required.

Once a book is completed, it is reviewed by copyeditors and then passed along to proofreaders. Copyeditors search for errors in spelling, word usage, grammar, and context. Proofreaders look for any discrepancies between the edited manuscript and the final product.

EDUCATION

B.A./B.S. Recommended for
Lower-Level Positions
B.A./B.S. Required for
Upper-Level Positions

$$$ SALARY/EARNINGS

$20,000 to $30,000
$30,000 to $40,000

At the top of the editorial hierarchy at trade book publishers is the editor-in-chief, publisher, or editorial director. This individual is responsible for both editorial and business aspects of the enterprise: establishing the annual operating budget, working closely with editorial and marketing departments to set up editorial projects, and staying on top of sales feasibility studies. Ultimately he or she is the person who is held responsible for the quality of each book and how well it does in the marketplace.

Children's Book Publishers

EDUCATION
B.A./B.S. Recommended
B.A./B.S. Required

SALARY/EARNINGS
$20,000 to $30,000
$30,000 to $40,000

Children's publishing includes everything from picture books to teen fiction and non-fiction. This category constitutes an important segment of book publishing and has only been treated as a separate entity since just after World War I.

Although children's book publishing is similar to adult trade publishing, there are some important differences. One lies in the added importance given to the visual aspect of children's books. The younger the intended audience, the more important the visual content of the book. Often authors are not capable of illustrating their own books. In this case, the publisher usually assigns an illustrator, and the author and illustrator split the customary 10 percent royalty.

Another distinction lies in the marketing of the books. Adult books are usually sold in bookstores, whereas a high percentage of children's hardcover book sales come from school and public libraries.

Most publishers plan schedules that allow publication of children's books for spring and fall, roughly to coincide with the beginning of school semesters.

Paperback Publishers

EDUCATION
B.A./B.S. Recommended
B.A./B.S. Required

SALARY/EARNINGS
$20,000 to $30,000
$30,000 to $40,000

Trade book publishers often have paperback divisions. Though they occasionally produce original manuscripts, these divisions usually look for suitable hardbound books to publish as paperbacks. Sold mainly through newsstands and retail outlets, paperbacks are generally divided into two main categories: trade and mass market. Trade paperbacks are usually sold in retail stores, department stores, and bookstores. Mass market paperbacks are usually sold via local and national distributors, the way magazines are sold.

The editorial staff of a paperback publisher is dedicated to searching for appropriate books already in print that are good bets to do well in paperback. After making choices, editors focus on improving the manuscript and the visual aspects of the book.

Publishers who produce new manuscripts employ editors who are skilled at creating and developing innovative and interesting ideas and assigning them to writers who can do them justice. Editors who deal with new submissions may also be assigned to read unsolicited manuscripts and deal with authors and agents.

EDUCATION

B.A./B.S. Recommended
B.A./B.S. Required

$$$ SALARY/EARNINGS

$20,000 to $30,000
$30,000 to $40,000

Textbook Publishers

Textbook publishing is an important area of educational publishing, and includes all books intended for elementary, secondary, or university classrooms. Products include hardbound and paperbacks, maps, manuals, dictionaries, audiovisual materials, encyclopedias, and other reference materials.

Textbook production may exist as a separate publishing division or it may be exclusively what that company is engaged in. For instance, NTC Publishing Group, the publisher of this book, produces trade books in addition to secondary and college textbooks.

Differences between textbook and trade publishing produce editorial distinctions. The risks in textbook publishing are much greater because a new high school textbook, for instance, could translate to an outlay of $250,000, whereas a trade book that doesn't do well may be compensated for with other books available at the time (that is, books that are on the "list").

At the top of the editorial hierarchy in textbook publishing are executive editors, whose primary responsibilities lie in planning and management. Answering to him or her are senior editors, project editors, associate editors, assistant editors, and editorial assistants. Many staff members work together to produce one project, such as a new math series. In most cases, such projects are large, since they usually call for the creation of a book for every level from kindergarten through eighth grade, in addition to teacher's editions and ancillary materials. When more help is needed, established authors, specialists in the field, and freelance writers are called in on a temporary basis. All project members will be involved in reading, creating, editing, and proofreading. Other staff employees who will work on the project include production editors, designers, and artists.

Upon completion of the project, the project editor may be involved in marketing the new books in the form of seminars and other meetings, where the series is explained and promoted to sales staff and state school committees.

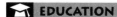 **EDUCATION**

B.A./B.S. Recommended
B.A./B.S. Required

$$$ SALARY/EARNINGS

$20,000 to $30,000
$30,000 to $40,000

Book Clubs

Book clubs appeal to certain segments of the population who are known to be interested in particular topics, such as mysteries, writing, gardening, or crafts. Book clubs market books published by other companies (and sometimes publish original manuscripts themselves).

The staff at book clubs includes editors of varying ranks, copy editors, editorial assistants, and proofreaders, who check all copy for grammar, style, punctuation, and accuracy–just as they do in all areas of publishing.

Editors of book clubs pore through the thousands of submissions they receive every year and make decisions about which ones to feature as book selections. There are three main distinctions between their responsibilities and those of trade publishing editors:

1. They usually focus on books that are already published, thus they avoid having to deal with the many thousands of unsolicited manuscripts that authors submit.

2. Book club editors don't usually do manuscript editing.

3. Book club editors don't usually deal directly with authors or agents, they deal with subsidiary departments. However they are responsible for their choices and how well they do for their companies.

In addition to staff editors, book clubs sometimes use outside readers to critique book club possibilities.

University and Small Presses

University presses are always on the look-out for outstanding works, particularly in the medical, technical, scientific, or business areas. College professors are often sought out to write those books and are awarded contracts by sponsoring editors. The author and editor then work together to produce the best book possible. Editorial assistants and copy editors may also be employed to upgrade the manuscript.

Small presses operate in the same manner as larger ones, except with limitations in scope and finances. Sometimes small presses evolve when authors decide to self-publish and then add additional books to their publishing list. In some cases, a small press will be the first to recognize the importance of a book. For example, *The Hunt for Red October*, Tom Clancy's first novel, was originally published by the Naval Institute Press, which is a small press.

Desktop publishing has promoted the expanse of small press publishing, and you can now publish a book quickly and credibly for a relatively small sum.

Religious Presses

Organized along the same lines of other publication enterprises, religious presses focus on issues of a religious or theological nature. Editors are responsible for creating ideas, choosing manuscripts or writers to complete them, and overseeing all stages and phases of the book. Authors are often clergy members who are not trained as writers and thus may require additional editorial help.

TRAINING FOR BOOK PUBLISHING PERSONNEL

A bachelor's degree is generally required for entering this field. Sometimes employers accept a broad liberal arts background;

usually they seek communications, journalism, or English degrees. Your chances will be further improved if you study at programs such as the University of Denver's Publishing Institute or take courses at the University of Chicago or New York University. Experience in the form of internships, publishing related jobs, writing experience, and published articles are all assets that may place you ahead of others vying for positions. Additionally, candidates must have a strong writing ability, computer knowledge, research and organizational skills, and the ability to meet deadlines.

JOB OUTLOOK

Jobs opportunities will be greatest in cities such as Chicago, New York, Boston, San Francisco, Washington, D.C., Los Angeles, Boston, and Philadelphia, where larger numbers of book publishers are headquartered. *The Occupational Outlook Handbook* expects opportunities in this field to increase about as fast as average for all occupations through the year 2005.

SALARIES FOR BOOK PUBLISHING PERSONNEL

It is reported that writers and editorial assistants can expect an average salary of $20,000 annually. According to a recent study by *Publishers Weekly*, copyeditors average $35,000; editors average $38,000; acquisitions editors average $55,000; executive, senior and managing editors average $62,000; and editors-in-chief or editorial directors average about $73,000 a year.

RELATED FIELDS

The communication skills and background necessary for success in book publishing are also important in newspaper publishing, magazine publishing, electronic media, and public relations.

INTERVIEW

Mary Elise Monsell
Children's Book Author and Teacher

Mary Elise Monsell is the author of seven children's books. Her first book, Underwear, was chosen favorite picturebook by the children in Wisconsin. She earned an M.A.T. from National-Louis University and teaches writing and reading classes at Oakton Community College, as well as conducting children's and teacher's workshops.

What the Job's Really Like

"Food's good and you meet interesting people."

Wrigley Field was hot. But it was hotter in the bleachers. The rock hopper penguin detective Mr. Pin and his friend Maggie were sitting under the scoreboard, watching the Cubs.

—From *The Spy Who Came North From the Pole*, by M. Monsell.

"It's great being a children's book author. I get to visit interesting places and meet unusual people."

"You must work for the museum," said Mr. Pin. "Yes," said the man in white. "I am a paleontologist. I study dinosaurs. I am Professor Hugo Femur."

—From *Mr. Pin: The Chocolate Files*, by M. Monsell.

"And *most* of the time, the food is quite good, with one or two exceptions ..."

The glass door of the case had been forced open, so the penguin detective was able to dip his wing into the case and lightly touch a chocolate egg. He preened his wing, then announced, "There is something wrong with this chocolate."

—From *Mr. Pin: The Chocolate Files*.

"There are highs and lows as in any business. And there are uncertainties one tries to meet with an abundance of chocolate and a good part-time job."

It had been days since Mr. Pin left his home at the South Pole to be a detective in Chicago.

—From *The Mysterious Cases of Mr. Pin*, by M. Monsell.

"My day begins with my family–two boys, two gerbils, two lizards. Once the boys are at school, I am able to write for a few hours. Sometimes I don't. When I'm not writing, I visit schools, teach at a junior college, volunteer, or give speeches. I also write letters, edit manuscripts, return phone calls, and, in general, do the business of being a writer. I write on weekends, late at night, in waiting rooms, and in grocery lines. In short, I write anywhere. I get crabby if I don't write. *Mr. Pin* was written at my dining room table with intermittent screen door slams and cries of 'Mom!!!' punctuating my literary pursuit."

How Mary Elise Monsell Got Started

"I think it has always been this way, the wanting to write part. Since I was seven, I knew I wanted to be a writer, but if that didn't work, I'd be a philosopher. The less lofty goal triumphed. That success began with a somewhat haphazard approach where I randomly submitted stories to publishers. Then I decided to treat my writing as a business. I researched children's books, publishers, and made up a schedule of writing 10 books and submitting each of them to 10 publishers. The real success was believing I could do it. The first book in this plan was *Mr. Pin*. It was accepted by the third publisher I sent it to. Today it is an IRA/CBA Children's Choice. *Mr. Pin* has become a series, and is published in paperback and sold in book clubs.

"I find that as an artist I need to continually reassure myself, despite small victories, that what I am doing is right. It would be nice to drive a car without rust, I think. The truth is that writing for children is what I do best. I think I would be just adequate at another, less creative career. Besides, with a quick flick of a few keys, I can make any event happen or resolve, involving any number of obscure characters, such as Orfo the Orangutan, Mort Chissel (the fossil man), Dr. Herbert Rootrot, among others."

Expert Advice

"There is a little insanity to this profession along with dogged hard work. I'm not sure how to best prepare oneself for the art of writing for children. I began with a degree from Northwestern's Medill School of Journalism, taught Montessori school for several years, and spent a lot of time with my two boys. But I think the best preparation is to lead a good life. Read a lot, visit places. Ask many questions. Think about things. Why do people say things that are untrue or unkind? What would happen if they didn't? How would they change? What do I wish for? What does a child wish? What do you feel when the worst thing happens? How did I feel when I lost someone in my life? How would I react as a child? What would make it better?

"I draw from my own life experiences, the sorrows and joys, and how I somehow appear in the next life event, somewhat wrinkled, a little worn, but knowing more. It's really no mystery why I do what I do. I love to make children laugh and make them feel better, to tell them stories from my heart in the voices of wood turtles and penguins. You see, it's the creatures I create that do all of the thinking. I merely record what they tell me to write. And if you buy into *that* fantasy, you may have a career waiting for you writing for the most wonderful of readers: children."

INTERVIEW

Dorothy Haas
Children's Book Author and Editor

In her 27 years as a children's book editor, Dorothy Haas has been responsible for the publication of more than 600 books. As an author, her publications for juveniles number more than 50 books. Among the most recent are: Burton and the Giggle Machine, (Bradbury Press, 1992); Burton's Zoom Zoom Va-Rooom Machine, (Bradbury

Press, 1990); The Secret Life of Dilly McBean, (Bradbury Press, 1986); and Peanut Butter and Jelly, (a series published by Scholastic; books 7, 8, and 9 published in 1990). Haas is listed in Gale Research's Something About the Author Autobiography Series (Fall 1993); Wilson's Sixth Book of Junior Authors and Illustrators; and Gale Research's Something About the Author, Contemporary American Authors, (new revision series, volume 20). Her work has been well-reviewed, including the following comments about Burton and the Giggle Machine: "The story develops with an undeniable sense of style and an irrepressible sense of humor" (Booklist). The book "... [sends] a powerful message that problem solving is hard work that can be both liberating and gratifying" (Kirkus). She was featured in the Book Links January 1993 issue, which saluted the good books of 1992.

What the Job's Really Like

"Novices or others who are not writers have no conception of the writer's craft. After you delve into it, you begin to assess all the skills that are necessary, and then as you gain expertise, you begin to acquire them. But no matter what level you're at, you're still learning. What you do can always be better. In fact, I believe if the new writer looks at his or her work and says, 'I can make this better,' he or she is already a writer. When a neophyte looks at something and says, 'Isn't this wonderful, I don't think it can be improved,' I suspect that individual may never become a truly fulfilled writer. What I am saying is, the working writer must have insight into the quality of his or her own work.

"When something is right I have a gut feeling, an inner sense of 'rightness,' that it's completed. If something is not right, a vague feeling of 'wrongness' nags somewhere at the back of my mind. It's easy to ignore that nagging little voice. I have learned to let it surface and pay attention to it. After working through revision after revision after revision, you will finally achieve your own gut feeling, that inner sense of 'rightness,' the feeling of satisfaction and completion that comes from knowing that the work has reached its potential and become what you want it to be."

How Dorothy Haas Got Started

"After graduating from college as an English major, I found the ideal position in my hometown, Racine, Wisconsin. I was hired as a summer assistant in the editorial department of Whitman Publishing Company (at the time an editing and publishing arm of a very large printer, Western Publishing), and was expected to proofread, plan pictures for children's books, and do odd jobs. With the atmosphere of children's books all around me, I decided to challenge myself by writing one. (Actually, I had written children's books in high school and received some encouragement). So, in my spare time on weekends and in the evenings, I did a picturebook about a puppy who was lost and later found with the help of a magnifying glass. Once I finished, I took it to the head of the editorial department and submitted it as *Little Joe's Puppy*. To my delight, the company decided they wanted to publish the book. And to make a wonderful situation even better, they then asked if I wanted to stay on as a permanent editor. Within two months of my college graduation, I had jumped into both fields.

"I worked hard as an editor by day and seized every spare moment to write after hours. Within a few years, I had done several more books for Whitman–picture books, a collection of biographies of famous scientists, and a novelette about Sir Lancelot. And all the time I was growing, both as an editor and as a writer.

"It was helpful for me to be following dual careers, because I became totally immersed in the field of children's books. I read all the classics. I went to the library and read everything there. I went to the bookstore to search out all the new books. I read everything that the well-known academics had to say on the subject of children's books. All of this was advantageous because pretty soon I began to have notions of what I thought was good and what I thought lacked something.

"On the other side of the coin, being an editor makes you question everything, and in writing it makes setting down a first draft a very difficult thing for me. I'm so critical I can hardly let the creative juices flow."

Expert Advice

"I would advise that you examine yourself, your needs, your strengths, your interests. Be flexible and willing to do many things, but build on your own assets. Don't try to be all things to all people.

"There are so many different kinds of writing and editing; you need to determine what is best for you. Are you interested in sports or science? Would you feel comfortable writing for a magazine, textbook company, advertising agency, or newspaper? Find out what you're best at and then seek out a position in that area.

"When you are starting out, read, read, read the kinds of things you want to write about. After reading everything out there, ask yourself some questions. Do you like the work? Do you dislike the work? Why? Then take a book you enjoyed and deface it with colored highlights by analyzing the passages you particularly liked. 'Oh, here's a good passage of dialogue,' you might say, or 'Here's how the author got from last week to this morning.' The passage of time is not easy to handle convincingly. Later, when you're having trouble showing that time has elapsed in your own story, you can look back at your marked-up book and see how the writer handled it. This practice can give you good pointers to implement in your own writing."

INTERVIEW

Carole Preston
Acquisitions Editor

Carole Preston is an acquisitions editor for a smaller book publisher in

a large city.

What the Job's Really Like

"Acquisitions editors become involved in the book development process early on. All of our book ideas are established in-house, so when an idea is conceived we find the freelancers, explain the concept of the book to them, negotiate money figures, and eventually hire them via agreed upon contracts. This is also true for illustrators.

"A big part of my job is doing research to find qualified people to handle the assignments we need to complete. Considerable time is spent negotiating the terms of contracts. We always have to keep on top of what people are getting paid, and stay aware of keeping within the budget we've been given. Sometimes it's hard to find people who are willing to work for what we can afford to pay. And if someone rejects the price or the job, I don't take it personally. If they ask for more money, I say I'll try and then I approach my superior. But the decision isn't in my hands.

"Usually I deal directly with writers, although sometimes it is an agent or, in the case of illustrators, a representative. If we were a bigger budget publishing house, then I'm sure I would be dealing with a much larger number of agents.

"Once the manuscript is written, it is turned in to me. I scan it over to make sure it's within the proper length and that it's pretty much what we wanted. In some companies the acquisitions editor does the initial edit on the manuscript when it comes in, but I hand it off to another editor who will do this.

"It's gratifying to make a direct contribution to the quality of the projects we are producing. It's challenging to search for the best people possible and exciting when someone signs on."

How Carole Preston Got Started

"This is something I've always known I wanted to do. I got involved in journalism as a freshman in high school and knew that I wanted to stick with that in college. My only problem was that I was torn between journalism and English. I chose English because I thought it would offer me broader opportunities. (I even considered law but decided to forego that for English). I completed my studies at the University of Illinois in Champaign, receiving a Bachelor's degree in English.

"In my freshman year of college I did an internship for a magazine, which kind of turned me off of publishing. It was for a very small company where there wasn't a lot of opportunity. Though I liked the job, everyone else was very unhappy. I considered giving up the whole industry and pursuing advertising instead. I took some advertising classes, but quickly decided that field certainly wasn't for me. It just seemed kind of meaningless.

I felt I wasn't really contributing anything to the world by writing toilet paper jingles. I decided I would try to get back into publishing.

"Subsequently, I got a job at a reference book publisher where I was a production assistant. At that point I decided I liked publishing as a career even though I had not yet found the right company for me. It struck me that making books was an honorable, enjoyable and important thing to do with your life.

"After I worked for the reference publisher, I moved to an educational textbook development house (a company that develops books for several publishers). Starting off as a proofreader, I did nothing but read for eight hours a day. Quickly I noticed my eyesight deteriorating.

"Luckily at that point the company was expanding into video and I moved into that department into a more developmental role. It wasn't a good fit for me, though, because I didn't know very much about that field. So I went back into production as an editor and eventually combined all my experience from the video development role and the editorial side into the job I have now."

Expert Advice

"The reality is that in order to get hired you need to begin with a college degree. This field is very competitive and not having a degree would be the first reason for being cut out of the running. It doesn't necessarily have to be in English, communications, or journalism, although a degree in one of those fields can help. Having a specialty subject or field of expertise is also a definite plus. For instance, if you want to work for a magazine and you're also really into cars, you can combine those two things to give you an advantage over other applicants. Medical editing, for instance, is a huge field that combines two areas of expertise. Internships are another must–be sure to complete at least one.

"People complain about salaries, but I think there are probably other fields that pay as little and are less rewarding. So although you're not going to start at the same salary that an engineer or an accountant would, I think it's probably comparable to what most other liberal arts majors would get at the entry level.

"Unless you just happen to live in a small town where there is a lot of publishing going on, it seems as if you are pretty much stuck in a big city atmosphere. For the maximum number of opportunities, go to New York.

"Look into joining professional associations, particularly if you're a recent graduate. They provide you with valuable educational and networking opportunities. Believe it or not–I found a *few* jobs that way."

INTERVIEW

Jan Mason
Senior Production Editor

Jan Mason is a production editor for a book publishing company located near a large city.

What the Job's Really Like

"Production editors act as liaisons between art directors, typesetters, editors, and any other in-house people. Once a manuscript is sent in and edited, the editor passes it on to me and I do a first reading. I concentrate on spelling, grammar, and content. Then I send it back to the editor with my recommended changes. The manuscript is then sent over to electronic publishing, our typesetting department. Usually they typeset a chapter and I route it to all the necessary people: the editor, the art director, and then all the higher-ups. Once that's approved, I give the typesetter the O.K. to typeset the rest of the book. After that, I make copies for my editor and then we both do another reading and exchange comments. From then on, it's a give and take between typesetting and me until the manuscript is sent to page make-up.

"With my recent promotion to senior production editor, I now train people and do second readings. This is how it goes. A book goes through several stages before it's completed. We get it as a manuscript and then, after it's typeset, the first thing we see is called a 'galley.' After the galleys are corrected, they're put into a dummy, which is a mock up of the way the actual pages will look. After it's dummied, it's keylined onto boards. Once it gets to boards, our policy is to have another person read it, because by that time you've read it four times. Chances are that you're likely to miss things.

"My job calls for me to attend some scheduling meetings. Also, I make sure that all deadlines are met, because we have a lot of important internal dates. If we miss the dummy date, for example, we're not going to meet the board date and then the book is not going to go out on time. Sometimes newer editors or art directors don't understand this vital concept, so as an older production editor, I try to nudge them along.

"I always enjoyed reading and now that I'm a senior production editor I'm responsible for doing a little bit more of the editorial work. I find I like making things right–correcting mistakes, finding inconsistencies. My goal is to make everything perfect, or at least the closest thing to it."

How Jan Mason Got Started

"I have a degree in English from Emory University. During my years there, I interned one summer at an advertising agency and one semester at a publishing company.

"Simple as it sounds, I got this job by answering an ad in the newspaper. After I responded, I was called in for an interview and was asked to take a test. It consisted of proofreading and 'what's wrong with this picture?' sections (in which you need to find the inconsistencies).

"I always wanted to be in this field. I was one of those people who helped everyone in college with their written assignments: reading, editing, providing ideas, and clearing up grammar. Everyone knew to come to me."

Expert Advice

"Find out what kinds of publications or books a company specializes in. If there is something in your background that you can list on your rèsumè or mention in your cover letter that clicks with what they do, you're more apt to receive a follow-up call. And make sure you use good grammar in your rèsumè and cover letters, because they're a good indication of your skills. I can't tell you how many come in that have typos or don't make any sense.

"It's important to have good people skills and a tough skin. A career in production means that you deal with everybody. It's often your job to smooth rough feelings.

"Since a great deal of your time will be spent at your desk working on your own, you need to be self-motivated and able to keep from getting bored. After all, you're not always going to get projects that interest you and each manuscript must be read and reread a number of times, so you must be able to sustain your concentration.

"For a job like this you have to be organized and, above all, *patient*. You can't let every little thing get to you. You are running on deadlines a lot and if you let the pressure get to you, you're going to drive yourself and everyone you work with crazy.

"Sometimes it's slow, sometimes it's hectic. And there are certain times when a close deadline means I have to work overtime, but I really don't mind it because I love the work that I'm doing."

INTERVIEW

Laura Larson
Copyeditor

Laura Larson has been a full-time freelance copyeditor for the past eight years.

What the Job's Really Like

"It's hard to define a typical day, but I am usually up very early in the morning. I like to get to work immediately and I continue for four to five hours. Then I'll take a run, work out, come back, eat something, read the paper, and enjoy my afternoon, which constitutes my down time. If I'm on a deadline or have a lot of projects going on simultaneously and need to make progress on several fronts, I'll work in the evenings as well. Since I often work on the weekends, I figure I work about 30 hours per week.

"One of the advantages that I saw to freelancing is that it would free up my time to use for other things that I feel very strongly about and want to pursue. For instance, I do a lot of volunteer work and enjoy furthering my education, and as a freelancer I have time to do that. I can't imagine ever going back to a nine-to-five sort of job. I really enjoy having the autonomy and freedom to arrange my time as I see fit.

"Usually my projects consist of copyediting very large book manuscripts, mostly college or graduate level textbooks, for the best textbook publishers, such as Prentice-Hall or MacMillan. (I also do editing of non-fiction books that are not textbooks.) The procedure I follow entails a lot of work with authors, which I love. Helping them produce the best writing and organization is very satisfying and allows me to get to know the manuscript material as well as the author knows it.

"One of my responsibilities is to make sure all the necessary permission statements are in order, so that art that's being reproduced or lengthy passages that are being quoted from other sources are accounted for. I also make sure that all the art is in place.

"At least 90 percent of my editorial work is done on computer now, so several years ago, I had to become more computer literate. I edit a book on the computer, the author reviews the manuscript and returns it to me, and I incorporate his or her revisions and corrections, additions, and answers to my questions. At the same time, I insert the design codes electronically so that when publishers receive the disks from me, they can slip them into the computer and out come the pages of the book. For the most part, the old step of having a typesetter is skipped. This saves the publisher time and money.

"Another thing I enjoy is that, since I get work from various publishers producing books on various topics, I'm forced to read a lot of very interesting materials that I probably would not have otherwise. I just finished a book on racial issues in the criminal justice system, which is an intriguing topic to me but I might not have read it for my own pleasure. However, I had to read it three times for my work, and I wind up learning a lot from reading so much. Another freelance editor and I kid about the vast amounts of trivia we pick up because we read so much in the course of our work!"

How Laura Larson Got Started

"I knew from about the age of four that I wanted to be a writer or work with books somehow. I had a love for literature and story telling, and all that was a very integral part of my growing up. So I never had a dilemma about what I wanted to study in college. After high school, I attended the University of Illinois in Champaign/Urbana, where the curriculum does not allow you to enter the College of Communications until your junior year. The first two years I majored in French and then became a journalism major, graduating with high honors.

"Following college, I accepted a position in a non-journalism related job for a few years at the University of Illinois library, where I had worked as a student. At the same time, I began to explore freelance options in the area. There were a few good-sized publishers, comparatively speaking, and I started to do some freelance proofreading and editing. In addition, I was also doing a lot of editing of graduate students' theses and dissertations.

"When I applied for my first job in publishing at the University of Illinois Press in their Office of Printing Services, I really exploited the little bit of experience I had. (It was a civil service position so I took the appropriate test and scored higher than anyone else). They decided to interview those who had the top three scores. During my interview I was told that they were impressed with my academic record and test scores but concerned by my lack of experience. Though in reality my experience was rather limited, I wanted the job and felt confident, so I assured them that I had experience editing and proofreading and would perform well in this position. I got the job and subsequently received a tremendous amount of hands-on experience and exposure to every facet of typesetting, editing, proofreading, and publishing. Most of my fellow employees had been in the business for many years and had a wealth of talent and information to offer me.

"After a year I applied for a job as an assistant editor at Human Kinetics Publishers, which is the largest sports publisher in the world. After a month they asked me if I would be interested in becoming a developmental editor in their scholarly and technically oriented books division. I jumped at the opportunity and found myself overseeing the entire production process, devising and correcting the freelance editing tests, hiring freelancers, as well as hiring and supervising an assistant editor who worked with me and another developmental editor in that area.

I got to work with a lot of authors from around the world, and since I know several foreign languages, I was able to communicate in their native tongues.

"At the same time, I was also becoming increasingly aware that the demands on all the editors' time was simply unreasonable. For instance the same copy editing schedule, (for example, three weeks), was allotted for every developmental editor for every kind of book–no matter if the manuscript was 200 or 1000 pages long. Seeds of frustration began to grow in me. The pay was also a lot less than what I had been making at the University of Illinois. I had been willing to make that concession because I knew that this job would be a tremendous education and a stepping-stone that would enable me to move up to freelance work. But after a while, I became dissatisfied to the point where I decided to quit and just jump in and try freelancing.

"As a result of this decision, I know what it's like to be absolutely dirt poor. I can remember distinctly having to decide between buying a gallon of milk or the Sunday paper because I didn't have enough money to do both. (I think I bought the paper). Champaign-Urbana is not exactly a publishing mecca of the United States, so I decided that it was time to move up to the Chicago area where there would be more opportunities. So I moved and began searching through the phone book, calling publishers in alphabetical order and inquiring whether they used freelancers. Though I learned that the great majority do not, there were a few who said, 'yes, send a resume.' (And one of those publishers became a client of mine and is to this day.) Actually, the main way I started getting work was through a former colleague of mine who had left and moved to Chicago before I did. This person recommended me to someone else and we worked on several projects together. A few months later, when someone from MacMillan Publishing contacted her asking for freelancers in the Chicago area, she gave her my name. It was just word of mouth recommendations. I've never done any self promotional marketing at all for my services. I don't even own business cards.

"The first year or two were very difficult. However, luckily for me every time I was getting to the point of utter desperation or self doubt, the phone would ring and I would be offered some fabulous job. It was just amazing serendipity. And now, after eight years, that's not even remotely a concern. I never have to hustle for work, I always have at least three projects going on at the same time."

Expert Advice

"I think it's possible for freelancers to 'have it all,' but you must never doubt yourself. In order to be successful, you must be curious, patient, and always have confidence in your abilities. I know a lot of people are afraid of not having a regular pay check and think they'll miss the interaction with colleagues. But I feel that I have a perfect balance between nice professional congeniality with colleagues without all the politicking that goes on in every office.

"I'd recommend that you not be afraid of taking on any sort of work that might be handed to you, even though you might think you're above it. At one point I was doing absolutely mundane proofreading–even literally proofreading the old fashioned way, where you read proofs out loud to someone else. It was low paying, absolutely torturous work, but I knew that I wasn't going to be doing that for the rest of my life and that this simply awful task would help me get something better. If you can think long term, every bit of experience builds on itself and will lead you to exactly where you want to be.

"One of the places I volunteer at is called *Streetwise*, a newspaper that's sold by homeless people in Chicago. As volunteer coordinator, I meet a lot of editorial volunteers who are doing this because they want to enhance their expertise as writers, reporters, illustrators, and/or photographers. By being open minded and enjoying the experience, they are building credits for their resumes and skills which will pay off handsomely for them later."

• • •

FOR MORE INFORMATION

For additional information, please consult the following:

American Book Producers Association
160 Fifth Avenue, Suite 604
New York, NY 10010-7000

American Society of Journalists and Authors
1501 Broadway, Suite 302
New York, NY 10036

Authors Guild
330 West 42nd Street
New York, NY 10036

Mystery Writers of America
17 East 47th Street, 6th Floor
New York, NY 10017

National Writers Union
873 Broadway, Room 203
New York, NY 10003

Society of Children's Book Writers
P.O. Box 66296
Mar Vista Station
Los Angeles, CA 90066

You may obtain a free copy of Griffin's *Signature*, which contains articles about producing and selling books, by contacting:

Griffin Printing and Lithography Co. Inc.
544 West Colorado Street
Glendale, CA 91204

Other useful books include *Opportunities in Publishing* and *Opportunities in Writing* (Lincolnwood, Ill: NTC Publishing Group).

CHAPTER 4

Radio and Television

OVERVIEW

The mediums of radio and television are brought to our homes, cars, offices, planes, and trains through the efforts of a large number of individuals, who perform a multitude of tasks at radio and television stations. These stations are usually divided into four departments, which include engineering, sales, administration, and programming. Though the news department may exist as a separate entity, it is usually contained within the programming section. This department is the home of many hardworking, busy journalists.

EDUCATION
RADIO
B.A./B.S. Required

TELEVISION
B.A./B.S. Required

$$$ SALARY/EARNINGS
RADIO
$12,000 to $20,000

TELEVISION
$20,000 to $30,000

EDUCATION
Post Graduate Recommended

$$$ SALARY/EARNINGS
$50,000 to $75,000+

Newsroom Staff

The number of people on staff will, of course, be determined by the size of the television or radio station. At larger stations, the jobs are more specialized; at smaller stations, everyone does a lot of things–or *everything*. For example, announcers may do their own writing and also sell advertising at smaller organizations.

The staff at a radio or television stations may include the following:

NEWS DIRECTORS. News directors are the CEOs of the news departments. Since they supervise the entire staff at the station, their positions are more managerial than journalistic. They have the final say on what stories will be covered and from what angle, and are thus involved in editing, reviewing, and approving all news film and videotape footage before it is shown to the public.

ASSISTANT NEWS DIRECTORS. Assistant news directors are usually in charge of the day-to-day operations of the news-room, including assigning stories to reporters and news writers, designating technical crews for particular projects, and choosing producers for individual news segments.

ANCHORS (NEWSCASTERS). Anchors are the individuals who serve as hosts or hostesses for the news programs. In order to develop a following of viewers, it is important for them to be attractive and charismatic. Yet although a pleasing personality and voice are important, a clear and impartial delivery of the news is the highest priority.

At larger stations, news anchors are not required to write their own stories. Smaller stations may not only require their anchors to write their own material, they may also be expected to be reporters. Even larger stations may ask their anchors to research, write, or rewrite a portion of the material being presented.

Anchors often conduct on-camera interviews and may host special productions.

ANNOUNCERS/DJS. Radio and television audiences enjoy getting to know radio and television announcers. Often called disc jockeys, since they may select and play recorded music, radio announcers often discuss local and world issues in a "talk show" forum; interview guests; and present news, weather, commercials, and sports. In some cases, they may research, write their own scripts, compose news stories, and create commercial copy. Where written copy is not used, "ad-libbing" is widely implemented. They may also be called upon to operate the control board and sell commercial time to advertisers.

Announcers must demonstrate split-second timing, and they often work irregular hours–two factors which may cause stress. However, most announcers feel that becoming known by the public, and performing interesting, creative work makes it all worthwhile.

WEATHER REPORTERS (METEOROLOGISTS). Weather reporters range from highly qualified, educated meteorologists to individuals with less formal training who have an overall likable manner, pleasant appearance, and good verbal acuity. Employed by local and major networks, as well as by The Weather Channel and cable stations, weather reporters gather daily information regarding weather conditions and present daily and long range weather forecasts. Since these forecasts are based upon wire service reports, local and regional governmental agencies, and national satellite weather services (and perhaps even their own weather equipment), weather reporters must have a great deal of expertise in operating sophisticated weather radar systems and their associated computer graphics, which are used to show temperature, barometric pressure, wind speed, humidity, and pollen count.

In addition, weather reporters are always looking for new and more interesting ways to present their weather reports.

SPORTSCASTERS, SPORTS DIRECTORS, OR SPORTS REPORTERS. Sportscasters operate much like other reporters, except that their focus is always sports-related. They are responsible for reporting on all sports and athletic events, doing play-by-play segments for television viewers, interviewing sports personalities, and developing sports feature stories. Often former coaches, newspaper sports writers, or sports figures, these radio and television journalists often travel extensively during specific seasons.

At smaller radio and television stations, sports reporters may be responsible for seeking out the sports news, organizing it, writing it, and presenting it to the viewers. They may also participate in local events, such as appearing at the opening of a new sporting goods store. At larger stations, reporters may be responsible for a specific sport or event or may be one of many sports reporters, all of whom report to a sports director.

As is the case with all television and radio personalities, it is important that sportscasters present an appealing and professional demeanor.

NEWS REPORTERS. Reporters who work in broadcast news (also referred to as "news announcers," "commentators," "analysts," or "newscasters") perform their jobs in much the same way that print reporters do. They gather the elements of a news story from a variety of sources, including interviews, personal observation, press briefings, various forms of research, and leads from wire services. They also decide from what perspective stories will be written (the "slant"), pursue follow-up stories of past events, and check out tips of newsbreaking stories from the public.

At smaller stations, where there may be no newswriters, reporters may also write the stories and even deliver them on the air. At larger stations, reporters may be specialists in one area or another, such as health or politics. In this case, newswriters work with reporters to develop stories.

Reporters may put in long, irregular hours, especially when a story is developing and must be followed up on–no matter *what* time it is.

Other Staff

Other staff members may include photojournalists, writers, assignment editors, and tape editors.

TRAINING FOR RADIO AND TELEVISION PERSONNEL

Students can begin to prepare for this type of work by spending time in campus radio or TV facilities and at commercial stations. Some regular or cable stations offer internships, co-op work programs, apprentice programs, or scholarships; all of these are excellent and valued avenues to pursue. Excellent experience can also be acquired in part-time and/or summer jobs in the field, and through public speaking or debate.

Although a college degree is not always mandatory, it is certainly preferred. The Accrediting Council on Education in Journalism and Mass Communication recommends that 75 percent of the coursework be in the area of liberal arts, and the remaining 25 percent in journalism, preferably in broadcast journalism. In this competitive field, you need to know as much as you can about as many areas as possible. You will invariably be called upon to use information you have acquired previously, so the more you know, the better. Keep learning!

You'll also need to have a voice that is perceived well by listeners, of course. Taped auditions are usually required by employers to determine how well an individual performs, particularly in front of the camera.

You can expect to begin your career in an entry-level position, such as production assistant, secretary, researcher, or field reporter. Those who show promise may be elevated to an on-air opportunity, but this is not likely to happen too quickly.

Announcers generally begin their careers on small stations in small cities, moving to larger stations and perhaps larger cities as they gain experience. Those entering this field should realize that relocation may be crucial to career advancement.

Announcers at smaller radio stations often operate transmitters, so a Federal Communications Commission (FCC) restricted radio telephone operator permit may be required.

JOB OUTLOOK

The number of people employed as announcers is expected to increase at the average level through the year 2005. This is due, in part, to the continued expansion of cable television systems. As is true of all media careers, however, competition will be keen. Chances for employment, especially for those new to the field, are better at smaller stations, where the pay is lower.

SALARIES FOR RADIO AND TELEVISION PERSONNEL

There is a wide range of salaries in this field. In general, television pays better than radio, commercial broadcasting pays more than non-commercial, and larger stations pay more than smaller ones (two to three times more, in the case of television).

A survey conducted by the National Association of Broadcasters and the Broadcast Cable Financial Management Association revealed a median salary of $17,000 per year for experienced radio announcers, $17,700 for news announcers, $18,000 for sports reporters, and $88,000 for news directors.

For television announcers, the median salary averaged $41,000. Weathercasters averaged $36,600 and sportscasters averaged $31,900.

RELATED FIELDS

A solid background in public speaking is the common thread that ties all of these careers together. Other positions that require this skill include salespeople, teachers, actors, interpreters, and public relations specialists.

INTERVIEW

Sylvia Perez
TV News Anchor

Sylvia Perez is a WLS-TV Channel 7 anchor in Chicago. She has worked in broadcasting since 1983.

What the Job's Really Like

"Being an anchor is really not the glamorous job everyone seems to think it is. That's because sitting behind the studio anchor desk is only a very small portion of the whole job. A typical day means *RUSH, RUSH, RUSH.* Since I don't get off the air until noon, I get a late start on whatever my assigned story is. It may be a story that a reporter from another station is covering and might have started much earlier. That means that I have to play catch-up from the start and work fast. I may only have a short time to put the story together, but I still must be thorough and make sure I don't omit any important details. Of course, if there's some important late-breaking news, I'll be assigned to that story, which may mean going out on the street, doing interviews, gathering all the facts, and then writing the story. The story is either presented live or as a self-contained piece for one of the newscasts–usually in the 5:00 or 6:00 P.M. news spot."

How Sylvia Perez Got Started

"I attended journalism school at the University of Oklahoma and began my journalism career in 1983. My first job was in my home town of Lawton, Oklahoma. I did morning news cut-ins and daily reporting. In 1984 I made the decision to move to another small station in Amarillo, Texas, because the Lawton station did not have live satellite units needed to provide live capabilities.

"What an exciting time of my life this turned out to be! I received a phone call from an agent who was familiar with my demo tape (a tape showing a sample of my work), who asked if I would like to be represented by that company. The company had already successfully forwarded the tape on to a station in Denver, Colorado, that was showing interest in me. With only six months experience in Amarillo, I moved to Denver to become a morning news anchor and weekday reporter. I had only worked in a small market and in a very short time I was headed to an exciting city with a medium-sized market and a very professional newscast.

"After a two-year stint in Denver, I started to feel the hours begin to take their toll. I had to arrive at 4 A.M. to write the news that I would present on the 6 A.M. show. That meant getting to bed really early so that I could get up at 2:30 A.M. and be at work on time. Needless to say, this was very difficult. In addition, I didn't see the possibility of upward movement. So I decided to move on.

"Incredibly, with no forewarning, I received a call from an NBC station. The voice on the other end of the phone said, 'I've seen your tape. Would you like to be a Houston weekend anchor?' He attempted to hire me over the phone but I flew out for an interview and decided subsequently it would be a good career move. I spent the next two years in Houston as medical reporter and weekend anchor. After that I decided that medical reporting was not for me and with the aid of an agent, I received a number of job offers. Two of the offers were in Chicago. My ultimate choice was WLS-TV, where I was hired as a weekday reporter and weekend anchor. Happily in September, 1992, I became the co-anchor of Eyewitness News with Linda Yu (at 11:30 A.M.), the first newscast in Chicago anchored by two women."

Expert Advice

"The reality of the job is that stations look for aggressive reporters who are not afraid to work hard. The career is demanding and extremely competitive. If you are not committed, you'll never make it. And you always have to be available–24 hours a day, 7 days a week. You must be eager to learn, since every day you are put in new situations that you must translate efficiently to the viewer. Sometimes you have to go on air live the minute you reach the scene of a newsworthy event, so you must really be able to think on your feet quickly.

"You need to be able to conduct effective interviews with people of all walks of life, and you must have the background and knowledge to put the story together into a cohesive and interesting form. And you must be able to deal with the death and destruction that all too often are central to the news story, while still maintaining your professionalism, asking the important questions with compassion and accuracy.

"Stations no longer want personalities who simply read the news. You must be able to go out on the street, get your hands dirty and work, work, work! In this profession, you have to be flexible and ready to handle almost anything!"

INTERVIEW
Carol Stein
Radio Talk Show Host

Carol Stein's one-hour program on WEAT radio in Florida is called "Business Opportunities With Carol Stein."

What the Job's Really Like

"Every Saturday I feature three business entrepreneurs–producers, entertainers, or marketing or public relations specialists–from all over the world. I find out how they got started, what problems they faced, what advice they would offer, and how success has changed their lives. My experience is that these people are kind, down-to-earth individuals who have worked hard to earn the respect of others.

"Many people want to get into the field but most are not aware of 99 percent of the effort I expend behind the scenes. Most are intrigued by my career and often say, 'Oh, you're so lucky; you meet people like Dave Thomas (founder of Wendys), you're invited to lots of great parties, your life is so exciting.' But they don't realize that part of the reason for going to functions and parties is to promote both the show and myself and to meet new people who would be interesting to have as guests. (I've never had anyone turn me down.) Unfortunately this makes my work week a seven-day experience. I always have to go, even if I'm tired. But since I love my career, I feel as if I'm not really working.

"I am involved in all aspects of the show: getting the sponsors, booking the guests, doing the research, creating interview questions, performing the interviews, and editing tapes. So for every hour that I'm on the air, there are 20 to 40 hours of preparation time that no one sees (and this is what makes the show so good). I study financial reports, perform other research at the library, visit other pertinent sites, read company literature, do anything I can to familiarize myself with the prospective guest. It is my goal to get to know my interview subjects well. Then I create new and different questions for each interview. As a result, I am often up until 2 A.M. staring at my computer thinking I still have hours of work to complete my task. But I feel it's worth it because I can guarantee my guests that they will have a good time and be asked solid business questions."

How Carol Stein Got Started

"My background is a bit unusual in that I did not major in communications. As an undergraduate I went to the Wharton Business School, where I majored in finance and electrical engineering. Then I went on to obtain my MBA at Wharton.

"Entering the world of business, I traveled all over the globe as a consultant for several Fortune 500 companies in a number of diverse fields. At the other end of the spectrum, I also had experience in cheerleading, modeling, aerobics, teaching, and acting. My mother is a public relations specialist and my father has a Ph.D. in chemical engineering and owns his own business, so I guess I'm a product of both worlds.

"When you have experience, you make contacts and projects come to you. But when you are first starting out you have two options. You can either try to get hired at a television or radio station, or you can approach a station with an idea for a show you wish to produce. At the beginning of my media career, when I was living in Washington, D.C., I produced and hosted a television show. This allowed me to learn every aspect of television and also gave me the opportunity to interview many high-level personalities, including President Clinton. When I moved to Florida, I took my television concept and adapted it to radio. Though I had a lack of media experience at the time, I felt confident to handle all aspects of the project. My preference was to approach it that way, so that I could become familiar with all aspects of this business–producing, being on the air, hiring talented individuals, marketing, selling, editing, and everything else. As a result, I know how to work the camera, do audio, set up lighting. I write scripts. I know how to do graphics. I can work in front of a computer performing all the digital animation."

Expert Advice

"In this business you've got to be confident about your abilities and able to take rejection. Since the commodity you are 'putting out there' is *you*, it's hard not to take it personally when you are criticized, because it feels personal. But you have to believe in yourself and what you do so passionately that you are willing to keep trying and to endure–no matter what. You must be willing to commit to the time and effort and be patient until you are able to realize your dream.

"You must also be prepared to do whatever is necessary to achieve success. For instance, my job requires that I do a lot of selling; whether it's calling up to secure a guest for a show, talking to sponsors, or promoting a newspaper article about me or the show.

"It's important to remember that as a talk show host, the people you are interviewing are the stars, so it is your responsibility to get them comfortable enough so they can shine. Within them are the stories that people want to hear, so you need to keep *your* ego in check. If you're truly a good person who cares about others, people will trust you and feel comfortable with you. And if you're ethical and honest, you'll establish the right kind of reputation, which will stay with you throughout your career.

"One of the best parts of this career is that I'm excited by my work every day. I'm never bored–I meet many interesting, wonderful people, some of whom have become my friends. They encourage me and continually expand my sphere of knowledge. It's like getting my MBA every day!"

INTERVIEW
Brian R. Powell
Radio Personality/DJ

Brian R. Powell has been a radio personality and DJ on WCIL-FM radio in Carbondale, Illinois, for the past two years. His show is featured from 3:00 in the afternoon until 7:00 P.M.

What the Job's Really Like

"For me, this job is really quite informal and simple. I come in about an hour early and read as much of the newspapers as possible: the *Chicago Tribune*, the *St. Louis Post Dispatch*, *Southern Illinois*, and a couple of other smaller local papers. I look through them to familiarize myself with what is newsworthy–locally, regionally, and nationally. This is important, because I frequently receive phone calls when we're on the air from people wanting information about things that are going on in the world.

"We also receive trade publications published by record companies, which provide a wealth of information about music and the bands that we're playing. So I'll look through those as well.

"When it's actually time to go on the air, I go into the studio to select the music to play. Since we're a top-40 station, most of the music that we present repeats itself regularly about every four or five hours. The newest music is played most often. But since I'm also able to play selections of my own from the music that's provided in the library, I'll browse through there looking for songs I haven't played recently or something that looks interesting. Once I've made my selections, I organize the order of the songs so that the music is presented in a pleasing sequence and avoids abrupt changes.

"Usually the DJ who's on before me will pull the commercials that I need for the first hour of the show. So when I arrive each day, there is a stack of those on the cart ready for me. Most of the commercials are pre-recorded; but I do have some 'live reads.' These are fun because I can really ham it up. And I have responsibility for organizing the commercials into what we call 'top sets' or groupings, to make sure competitors are not played back to back (for instance, playing an ad for Coca Cola and then one for Pepsi).

"On occasion, I conduct brief interviews. I'm always free to proceed with such projects if I feel they would make 'good radio.' For instance, we recently had an interesting situation involving George Harrison's sister, who used to live in a house in southern Illinois. Back in 1963, before the Beatles ever came to America, George Harrison visited and stayed with her in that home. Not only that, he played a few songs on guitar in one of the local restaurants in town. Subsequently, this house was sold to the Illinois Department of Mines and Minerals who wanted to tear it down. This became a controversy, with people taking one side or the other. Since there was considerable local interest in this issue, I did a number of live interviews with some of the people involved, including Louise Harrison herself. In the end, the house was preserved.

"Much of what comes out of my mouth is not pre-scripted. What I say is whatever feels right to say at the time. In general, I try to minimize my speaking and emphasize the music, since I feel most people are listening at work or in their cars and have a desire to hear music–not talking."

How Brian R. Powell Got Started

"As a sophomore in high school, I was actually flunking English. My teacher took me aside and said, 'You know Brian, you are articulate and have a nice voice. You should try out for the high school radio station.' I had no idea that such a thing existed but I decided to check into it. Before I knew it, I had completed an audition and was doing a five-minute sportscast every day. Joyfully, it soon dawned on me that I could pursue this as a career (though I didn't know how to go about it at that point).

"I worked in high-school radio for three years and gained a substantial amount of experience in proper breathing techniques, how to present myself, technical aspects of the business, and other performance and behind-the-scenes endeavors, such as writing and editing.

"When I was a senior in high school I had an electronics teacher who was also chief engineer for WBBX, a suburban radio station in Highland Park, Illinois. He was able to get me a part-time job at the station for a whopping $2.30 an hour. After a stint in radio sales, I enrolled at Southern Illinois University, where I secured a job at SIU's radio station, WSIU. The classes that I took in radio and television were helpful, but my hours at the radio station provided a wealth of information. I settled in to enjoy my radio years there.

"Following this, I got a part-time position at WHBI in Heron, where I worked my way up to the prestigious morning position. While there, I increased my knowledge further and gained experience in doing play-by-play (the most difficult job in broadcasting). After about three years, I secured the morning position at WTAO in Murphysboro, just 10 miles away.

"Circumstances pushed me out of the radio business for a few years, until I moved back to Carbondale in 1992 and found my way to WCIL-FM. When I first came to the station I was assigned the overnight shift from 2 A.M. until 6 A.M. Then I volunteered to take the 10 A.M. to 2 P.M. slot for a vacationing DJ (and for a while I did both shifts). As a result, I impressed the general manager and won the afternoon spot. I'm happy with this time slot, because I get to sleep as late as I wish, whereas morning DJs must wake up at 4:30 or 5:00 A.M. Another bonus of this job is that I don't have to get dressed up; I frequently arrive at the station in sweatpants and a T-shirt and open-toed sandals. Most of the time I'm not seen by anybody, unless we have a radio tour on the calendar.

"I enjoy meeting the touring elementary and high school students. Often they have a preconceived notion of how complicated a radio station must be and I have the opportunity to teach them about how simple it all is. The one negative aspect to these occasions is that I don't get to enjoy the privacy I usually have. When I'm alone in the radio room, I feel I have the freedom to take chances, let my mind go, and be creative with no one staring at me. I want to be known–but not *well* known. Television is a totally different medium. Those involved in TV understand that since their physical image is commonplace, they can't go out in public without being recognized and possibly approached. In radio, my friends know who I am, but I don't have any pretenses about being famous.

"My ultimate goal is to do radio in Chicago, although I'd consider Milwaukee or St. Louis. The longer I am involved in radio, the more I realize I still have a way to go in perfecting my craft. But I'm very willing to put in the time and energy to accomplish this because I really enjoy what I'm doing."

Expert Advice

"If you are interested in a career in radio, the first thing you should do is make the radio a priority: listen to the DJs, what they say, and how they say it. Also be aware of what they *don't* say. When I was first starting out, I would try to repeat exactly what the DJ was saying right after it came out of his mouth, using the very same pacing and inflection. Try doing this–or any kind of performing for that matter–in front of an audience.

"In terms of classes, focus on English. It worked for me. I had B+s by the time I graduated. Also concentrate on journalism, psychology, and my personal favorite–political science. They complement radio work by sharpening your mind, thus allowing you to process information and think more quickly 'on your feet.' These qualities are vital to success in radio.

"Perhaps the most important advice I could offer is to be prepared for failure because if you are prepared for that, you will definitely be prepared for success."

INTERVIEW

Jerry King
Foreign Correspondent

Jerry King served as a foreign correspondent for ABC-TV in a variety of countries for over 15 years.

What the Job's Really Like

"As a foreign correspondent, you have to be able to function in a variety of circumstances. During my career I've been in Northern Ireland, Viet Nam, Lebanon, Afghanistan, Somalia, Iran, Iraq–the list goes on and on. In these situations you have to exist without the creature comforts of home and also be creative and quick thinking. I've been in Beirut cut off from all outside contact for weeks on end–without telephones or any other form of communication. When we filmed scenes we sometimes shot them with two cameras, hoping that at least one roll of film would make it out of the country.

"Foreign correspondents must rely on local journalists–the people who live and work in the area. When I was living in Germany, for example, when Helmut Kohl wanted to say or do something he didn't exactly call *me* up; his people called up the local reporters and got the word out though them. Maybe afterwards I could go back and get a particular slant or ask some specific questions, but my original information came from other journalists. The only exception is if you're on the spot at a breaking story, a hijacking for instance, where you can observe first-hand what is happening. I was lucky–in Poland I had a translator, a secretary, who knew Lech Walensa personally, so we had more access to him than some of the other journalists. I also had a cameraman in Lebanon who on Christmas day went around taking cookies to all the gunmen in the front lines because he wanted to be their friend. He once told me that if you're caught some place with a group of, shall we say, 'bad people,' you should always shake hands and keep shaking hands because they don't like to shoot you when they're shaking hands.

"At one point I was the first network television correspondent to come out of Warsaw after martial law was declared. We had been cut off so securely there from outside contact that the only thing we could hear was the BBC World Service shortwave broadcast. As time marched on, I thought the world had lost interest in the story, because the situation had not changed much. But when I was suddenly able to make my way out of the country by train, I was amazed how much interest there was. ABC flew me to London quickly, arranged for me to board a Concord headed for New York, and the next day I appeared on the 'David Brinkley Show,' 'Sunday Morning,' and 'Good Morning America.'

"I've seen humanity at its best and at its worst. As a foreign correspondent you are allowed to meet some pretty interesting people and witness some really fascinating things. On the other hand, there's also a tremendous boredom factor, sitting around in places like Baghdad where you're not allowed to do anything but wait. Getting through those days is not easy. And there are many times when you put in long hours, researching, interviewing, writing, and rewriting your stories. Though being a foreign correspondent certainly involves hard work, it is incredibly enjoyable."

How Jerry King Got Started

"My desire was to become a teacher; I was going to teach physical education. I've always been involved in sports. In Canada I spent one year at the university but unfortunately didn't do well in chemistry and physics. Since these were both requirements for my major, I was afraid I might be taking those classes every year forever. So I got into broadcasting and began doing sports in Canada, particularly hockey. Then I moved to Bermuda, worked there fashionably for the summer doing a radio DJ show and news, and television sports, and then moved to England and began working for United Press International in their radio/audio division from 1968 to 1971. In 1971 I switched over to ABC radio; from 1971 to 1975, I worked there as a freelance radio journalist. That led to a television correspondence job in Germany in 1975. Late that year I went to Beirut, where I worked for five and a half years before returning to the United States. Back in the United States I received a call from some friends overseas saying they needed a correspondent. Was I interested in coming over? I conferred with my supervisors in New York and they were thrilled that I wanted to go back. So I went to Germany and got involved in all the upheaval in Berlin.

"I didn't have the typical journalistic training. I got mine, as the old clichè goes, 'on the street.' I became a foreign correspondent by being overseas, being available, having some idea of how to write English–just doing it and gaining on-the-job experience."

Expert Advice

"I think aspiring journalists today would be well disposed to prepare themselves in areas like history, literature, English, law, economics, anything that will give them a solid background in a specialty–and then study journalism. Anybody can write, but that doesn't make you a good writer. I don't think you train to be a foreign correspondent (unless you study Russian or Chinese or something like that). It kind of grows out of what you want to do."

• • •

FOR MORE INFORMATION

For a listing of schools that offer courses and programming in broadcasting, contact:

Broadcast Education Association
1771 N Street N.W.
Washington, DC 20036

For additional information on broadcast news careers, contact:

Radio-Television News Directors Association
1717 K Street N.W., Suite 615
Washington, DC 20006

For general information on the broadcasting industry:

The National Association of Broadcasters
1771 N Street N.W.
Washington, DC 20036

For job listings, obtain copies of the following trade publications: Radio & Records, Broadcasting Magazine, and a pamphlet from the American Federation of Television and Radio Artists (AFTRA).

Further information on the field can be found in:

How to Launch Your Career in TV News, by Jeff Leshay, NTC Publishing Group, Lincolnwood, IL, 1993.
Opportunities in Television and Video, by Shonan F. R. Noronha, NTC Publishing Group, Lincolnwood, IL, 1993.

CHAPTER 5 Advertising

OVERVIEW

"The breakfast of champions," "Where's the beef?," "When it rains, it pours"–such phrases are familiar to most of us because of the effective work that advertising specialists have been performing for years. Some consider this phenomenon a nuisance that interrupts television programming and encourages people to buy products that may or may not be best for them. Others look upon it as a great public service. A dominating force in our society, mass-media advertising is a multi-million dollar industry dating back to the invention of movable type in the mid-1400s.

ADVERTISING AGENCIES

Virtually every type of business makes use of advertising in some form, often through the services of an advertising agency. The American Association of Advertising Agencies (the 4As) defines an advertising agency as "a service company that earns its income from planning, creating, producing and placing printed advertisements and broadcast commercials for its clients." Agencies may also offer additional services, such as market research, sales promotion, television programming, and public relations.

Agencies that are diversified and handle many kinds of advertising are called "full service advertising agencies." Other, more specialized agencies, may handle only one area, such as direct marketing.

An advertising agency may consist of only one employee or perhaps several thousand. Salaries will tend to be higher for those employed at bigger full-service agencies, because plum accounts like Coke or Charmin are more likely to engage larger advertising agencies.

Many people think the world of advertising is glamorous and exciting–and certain aspects can be. However, as Karen Cole Winters explains in Your Career in Advertising, "If you go into advertising expecting a constant whirl of fun and excitement, you'll probably be disappointed."

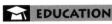 **EDUCATION**
B.A./B.S. Required

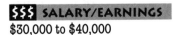 **SALARY/EARNINGS**
$30,000 to $40,000

Agency Staff

The work at each agency is frequently divided among several individuals or departments, which usually include the following:

• Account executives, who make sure that the clients' work is completed satisfactorily and on time. Account executives must be savvy about their agencies and aware of each client's desires and needs. Their responsibilities lie more in the business arena rather than in the creative aspects of the business.

• Art directors, who must be able to effectively present a theme or idea in convincing visual form, through illustration, color, photography or cinematography.

• Creative directors, who supervise all employees and oversee all activities in the agency. At the top of the hierarchy, creative directors must have creativity, people skills, and solid business acuity.

• Marketing researchers, who seek to determine what kind of audience would be interested in a particular product or service, why they are interested in the product, and how the public is reacting to advertising campaigns already in place.

• Media people, who work in the department that ensures that commercials are aired on radio and television and that ads get into magazines and newspapers.

Other advertising positions include television producers, print production managers, graphic artists, illustrators, photographers, freelance writers, print production personnel, and traffic managers.

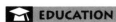 **EDUCATION**
B.A./B.S. Required

$$$ SALARY/EARNINGS
$30,000 to $40,000

Advertising Copywriters

What do Bob Newhart, Cornelia Otis Skinner, and Sinclair Lewis have in common? All of them served as advertising copywriters—the real creative forces behind advertising campaigns.

Advertising copywriters are responsible for the jingles and slogans that go around and around in our heads. They are the creative geniuses who dream up the words for commercials and advertisements and conjure up the themes for advertising campaigns. Copywriters may also be responsible for creating articles about products or services, sales promotion materials, public relations items, billboards, and promotional brochures.

Aspiring copywriters should be prepared for very long hours. In order to meet deadlines, a frantic daily agenda is often considered "part of the job." Copywriters usually begin their work by meeting with the client and/or account executive. After gathering as much information as possible, copywriters let their imaginations flow, looking for a slant on why a product or service is different from all others of its kind. Considerably more time will go into planning campaigns than will be spent on actually writing or drawing them.

Though copywriters may operate alone, they are usually members of creative teams that include art and creative directors (to whom they are usually responsible). Working together in brainstorming sessions, the creative team continually refines the advertising message.

Copywriters may write headlines, body copy, or both. The word "copy" refers to the printed message in newspaper or magazine ads, or the verbal part of a radio or TV commercial.

After completing a rough draft of the campaign, the copywriter must get client approval before proceeding any further. If the client is pleased with the results, the copywriter can go forward. If not, it's truly back to the drawing board.

Entry-level employees can expect to begin their tenure as junior copywriters. They will be expected to compose advertising ideas, participate in the writing of advertising copy, and develop sales and merchandising tools. Openings may exist in department stores, public relations companies, advertising concerns, or media and trade organizations.

TRAINING FOR ADVERTISING SPECIALISTS

Most employers will expect applicants to have a college degree. For those who aspire to become account executives, an MBA is especially important. Many schools offer programs in advertising, and a number of top advertising agencies offer in-house training programs for copywriters and account managers.

Since copywriters deal with a wide cross-section of ideas and concepts, a general liberal arts background in combination with business is particularly valued. Courses in such subjects as economics, history, journalism, marketing, advertising, math, social sciences, speech, literature, business administration, human relations, and creative writing are recommended.

Copywriters need the skills that all writers should have–the ability to produce clear, concise prose. Therefore, writing experience in the form of published articles, participation in school, church, or yearbook publications, local newspapers, internships, or radio or television studios are all worthwhile endeavors.

Candidates should prepare a portfolio containing three ads from two or three previous advertising campaigns. These can be class assignments or real ads from a client or job. If you have no advertising experience at all, present potential employers with samples of your writing (hopefully published).

JOB OUTLOOK

Advertising is a fiercely competitive field. If you cannot break in as a copywriter, you may be able to start as a secretary or administrative assistant. Be warned, however, that only a few individuals get the opportunity to advance to part-time or full-time copywriting jobs.

In general, job openings in the field of advertising are expected to grow as fast as average. Opportunities are generally greater at smaller companies, whose employees make more frequent moves to larger companies.

Madison Avenue in New York City is traditionally known as the advertising mecca, because of the large number of major advertising agencies located in this area.

SALARIES FOR ADVERTISING SPECIALISTS

There is a considerable range of salaries in this field, particularly in different regions of the country. The median annual salary in advertising agencies is about $35,000. Junior copywriters may start out with as little as $15,000; writers with senior status may earn $50,000 to $100,000, and even more as creative directors.

The larger the agency or account is, the higher the salary will be. The best locations for jobs in advertising are in cities: New York, Chicago, Detroit, Boston, Dallas, Atlanta, Los Angeles, and Minneapolis.

RELATED FIELDS

The skills required to succeed in advertising are those common to all careers in communications, particularly public relations, technical writing, or newspaper and magazine publishing.

INTERVIEW

Rosalind Sedacca
Advertising Copywriter

Rosalind Sedacca is a freelance advertising copywriter who started her own company, Rosalind Sedacca and Associates, over 10 years ago.

What the Job's Really Like

"Advertising copywriting requires extremely precise communication skills, excellent command of the English language, creativity, a great deal of responsibility, and considerable insight into marketing. One must also be meticulously organized and have expertise in proofreading and grammar.

"As a freelance copywriter you may be hired by advertising agencies, small businesses, or large corporations. All of them have different demands, but they share a common desire to communicate their business in its very best light. With this in mind, it will be your responsibility to find out as much as possible about the client's product or service. By asking a number of important questions, you must find out what is most marketable about their product or service and recommend the best type of advertising. They may think they need an ad or a brochure, for instance, but that might not be the best choice.

"A good copywriter always keeps in mind the differences between benefits and features. The features are the physical or mechanical aspects of a product or a service, such as the size, shape, or color. Benefits appeal to the buyer's emotions–it'll make you look younger, it'll make you look prettier, it'll make you smarter, it'll help you land a new job, it'll take inches off your waist–these are the reasons people buy. Thus in order to be a successful copywriter you must be cognizant of human nature and the psychology of selling.

"Once you have accumulated all the information possible, you have to put it together in as catchy a manner as possible. Keeping in mind your target audience, you set the tone of your copy to that particular market.

"One of the best features of this career is the autonomy I have in making my own hours and setting up my own schedule. My week is divided between working in the office at the computer and going out on appointments with clients and prospective clients. I also spend a lot of time on the phone, and regularly attend meetings of professional associations to network.

"Of course, there are frustrations, as there are in any business. You have to be willing to accept the fact that there's no one to take the brunt of all problems except you. You must be able to handle the deadlines, the demands, the details. At any time you may get calls from clients telling you they need their copy *tomor-*

row–and you've already promised two others you'd have *their* copy ready! Some nights I lie awake thinking about all the things I have to do.

"Another problem may be the business slumps, when you're just not getting as much work as you'd like. Cash flow problems may also surface. I try to get at least a 50 percent deposit as I begin and the remainder upon completion, but occasionally that balance doesn't arrive for two or three months–and I may have to write or call several times to make sure I get it.

"To attract clients, you must concentrate on networking. Most of my projects come through word-of-mouth referrals, which is wonderful. I haven't done a lot of advertising, although I know some very successful copywriters who have put classified ads in national publications and tried mailings and other means. I think you have to try whatever works. But in the beginning you must accept the fact that it's a slow process building a clientele, just as if you were a doctor or lawyer.

"Because no two days or two clients are alike, I can't imagine being bored. There's always stimulation with new challenges to your creativity. And when you see the results of your work in print, it's a wonderful feeling of accomplishment."

How Rosalind Sedacca Got Started

"In college I was very much into fashion and wanted to go to work at *Vogue* magazine. Although I wanted to work in the editorial department, the only opening they had at Conde Nast Publications was in the advertising department. So, of course, I accepted the position. My supervisor was the Creative Director of Circulation Promotions. Under her direction, I composed copy intended to solicit new subscribers (it was aimed at readers of *Vogue, Glamour, Mademoiselle, House and Garden* and *Brides Magazine*). I learned a great deal from my supervisor, and when she quit a year later, I was promoted to that position. I was 21. I subsequently left the company and went to an advertising agency that specialized in various types of direct response advertising. And later I moved from that into more general advertising.

"Over the past 20 years I've worked in every medium: print and direct mail, newspaper, magazine, radio, television, billboards, videos, and newsletters. This has been a challenge, as some of these categories require very different types of writing. For instance, there's a vast difference between the spoken word in a television or radio spot and the printed words of a brochure or a magazine ad. And public relations copy needs to be very 'clean' and editorial. Thus, you can't use the exciting adjectives that are desirable for other advertising media, such as magazine ads."

Expert Advice

"I recommend that anyone who is thinking of going into advertising do their homework by conducting research in the field. Part of that should include a study of your day-to-day mail to determine styles and help discover why things are done in a certain manner. For example, if you frequently receive 12-page letters selling a particular product, you might question the old adage that says that sales letters should be short. You can be sure that those pieces of mail wouldn't be out there if they hadn't proven to be successful. Most companies test and test and test again.

"It's important for prospective advertising copywriters to read some of the books by the masters, such as Ogilvy, who is considered the guru of advertising. You may then begin to get an understanding of how this field works. I'd advise you to then jump in and start trying things yourself. Give yourself assignments like, 'How can I perfect this ad? What would I say if this was my client? What can I do to create some pizzazz in this message?'

"I stress to beginners that you need to create a portfolio. If you're being hired for your writing skills, then obviously people will want to see what you've written. So it's smart to volunteer your services for small businesses just to secure some samples. Go to shopping centers and approach different kinds of stores and say, 'I'd like to do an ad for you at no charge. If you like the first one, would you hire me to do another one?' That way the company has nothing to lose and you will begin to accumulate printed samples of finished work.

"It's important to maintain a healthy ego. In the early days, my self-esteem would go up and down depending on how a client felt about my writing. And if three clients loved something and the fourth didn't, I would feel like a failure. You need to have a very strong sense of self-worth to know that, just because someone periodically criticizes your work, it doesn't mean there's something wrong with you.

"Along philosophical lines, I feel very strongly that the remainder of the 1990s through the 21st century is going to be the era of the small entrepreneur. Thus I recommend that anyone who is starting out should focus on the following questions. 'In what specific communications area can I become a specialist? What skills do I have to compete in the market place? And how may I remain as independent as possible to avoid being laid off or cast aside in the future?' The old idea of 'Stay on track in a corporation and you'll have a pension in 30 years,' just doesn't work. I was lucky I had the foresight to make the move to my own business because I was well-established by the time the slump of the late 1980s and early 1990s occurred. I was able to survive–and even thrive."

•   •   •

FOR MORE INFORMATION

The *Standard Directory of Advertising Agencies* will provide you with a list of agencies in a specific region.

Advertising Age
220 E. 42nd Street
New York, NY 10017

Advertising Club of New York
3 West 51st Street
New York, NY 10019

The Advertising Council Inc.
216 Madison Ave. 11th Floor
New York, NY 10022

American Advertising Federation
1400 K Street N.W., Suite 1000
Washington, DC 20005

American Association of Advertising Agencies
666 Third Avenue
New York, NY 10017

The Advertising Educational Foundation
Suite 1350, 666 Third Avenue
New York, NY 10017

International Advertising Association
475 Fifth Avenue
New York, NY 10017

Advertising Education Publications (3429 55th Street, Lubbock, Texas 79413), offers a book called, "Where Shall I Go to School to Study Advertising?" *The Standard Directory of Advertising Agencies*, known as the *Agency Red Book*, is another valuable resource; it lists more than 17,000 advertisers.

CHAPTER 6 · Public Relations

EDUCATION
B.A./B.S. Required

$$$ SALARY/EARNINGS
$20,000 to $30,000 (beginning)
$30,000 to $40,000 (average)
$40,000 to $50,000 (managers)

OVERVIEW

The concept of public relations is hardly a new invention. Indeed, it dates back to 1787, during the time of the Constitutional Convention. And in the 1800s, both the North and the South made use of the media during the Civil War in an attempt to persuade the populace to adopt their way of thinking.

The goal of public relations remains the same–to sway the public in a particular direction, or to build, maintain, and promote positive relationships between two factions: the agencies (or companies) and the public.

Public relations professionals may be self-employed or hired by public relations companies. They also find work in the PR departments of a variety of concerns, such as political parties, nonprofit organizations, hospitals, colleges and universities, trade unions, financial institutions, social service organizations, or clothing companies.

Business and industry rely on corporate public relations to educate the public about their products and services. And since nonprofit organizations do not generally advertise, they count on public service announcements provided by public relations professionals to get their message out.

PUBLIC RELATIONS WORK

The work of a public relations practitioner falls into six categories:

1. Research. This includes all of the preliminary work that is undertaken to ascertain the client's goals so that a plan to achieve them can be devised. Library research, client interviews, surveys, opinion polls, and collecting data are all part of this.

2. Program work. Once research is completed, a plan is set up based upon the findings.

3. Writing and editing. This may come in the form of press releases, presentations to clients, internal memos, reports, and magazine articles.

4. Special events. Included in this category are press conferences, special appearances, and autograph signings. All are carefully orchestrated to gain the greatest amount of attention.

5. Media placement. It is important to select the most important information to release, choose a good time to release it, and send it to the most advantageous receiver.

6. Fundraising. Fundraising is what sustains nonprofit organizations. Possible events include membership drives, direct solicitation, and benefit banquets.

Public relations professionals who work alone or in small companies may well handle any or all of the activities described above. Additionally, they may also perform advertising, marketing, and sales promotion duties.

Those who work as generalists in the field must be able to perform a wide array of duties at the same time. On any given week they may write press releases for one client, design a brochure for another, approach an editor for a third, meet with a talk show host for a fourth, implement a promotion for a fifth, set up a press conference for a sixth , put together a press kit for a seventh, work out the beginnings of a client contact for an eighth, and field media questions for a ninth!

Positions within public relations firms might include: public relations director or manager, account supervisor, account executive, account writer, public relations researcher, production supervisor, and public relations assistant.

Top managers or directors of public relations firms review campaigns and budgets, supervise personnel, and strive to secure new clients. Middle positions are filled by account executives. Entry-level office assistants answer phones, maintain files, do research, write media releases, and help with special events.

In the governmental arena, public relations specialists may be called press secretaries, communications specialists, or information officers. For example, public affairs specialists in the Department of Energy inform the public about proposed leases of offshore land for oil exploration. A senator's press secretary informs the elected official's constituents of his or her accomplishments and responds to questions from the media and the press. The press secretary schedules and appears at press conferences and issues statements from his or her superior.

Typically public relations specialists put in a 35- to 40-hour week, but overtime hours with no additional pay are common. Schedules often have to be rearranged to accommodate deadlines, speeches, meetings and other appearances–and to travel out of town. All of the above, particularly deadlines, may produce stress and possible burnout.

TRAINING FOR PUBLIC RELATIONS PERSONNEL

Although there is no defined training program for public relations specialists, it is wise to combine a bachelor's degree with some public relations experience, particularly in the form of an internship. Professionals in this field often have college majors in journalism, advertising, public relations, or communications. Some companies express a preference for someone with an MBA.

A common public relations sequence of courses includes the following: public relations principles and techniques; public relations management and administration, including organizational development; writing, emphasizing news releases, proposals, annual reports, scripts, speeches, and related items; visual communications, including desktop publishing and computer graphics; and research, emphasizing social science research and survey design and implementation.

Other courses that are valuable include: business administration, psychology, creative writing, advertising, journalism, sociology, and political science. Expertise in word processing and other computer applications and demonstrable skill in speaking and writing are also important. Writing for school, local, or religious publications provides valuable experience for prospective job seekers. Once samples accumulate, it is wise to organize them to form a portfolio of published work.

Membership in the Public Relations Student Society of America or the International Association of Business Communicators provides an opportunity for students to obtain information and make valuable contacts.

Some companies, particularly larger ones, provide formal training for their new hires. Smaller companies will tend to train their new employees on-the-job. Public relations specialists in larger companies gain more specialized experience, while those in smaller concerns gain more all-around experience.

Supervisory level positions are possible for those who show a willingness and capability to handle managerial situations. An individual might be hired as an entry-level employee (research assistant or accountant assistant), and be promoted to account executive, account supervisor, vice president, and ultimately senior vice president.

The Public Relations Society of America provides accreditation to those with a minimum of five years experience in the field who successfully pass a comprehensive six-hour examination (five hours written, one hour oral). The International Association of Business Communicators also has an accreditation program. Those who meet all requirements earn the designation of Accredited Business Communicator. Requirements include a least five years of experience in a communications field, successful completion of a written and oral examination, and approval of a portfolio of work samples.

JOB OUTLOOK

Although employment of public relations specialists is expected to increase about as fast as the average for all occupations through the year 2005, keen competition will continue as the number of applicants is expected to exceed the number of job openings.

Employment growth is expected to be limited as corporate reorganization and downsizing continue. This may provide greater opportunities for freelance workers to provide needed public relations services, since companies can then limit their support of full-time staff.

Though public relations businesses are scattered all over the United States, many are concentrated in New York, Chicago, Washington, D.C., and Los Angeles.

SALARIES FOR PUBLIC RELATIONS PERSONNEL

Median yearly earnings for full-time salaried public relations specialists average about $32,000. A recent College Placement Council salary survey found that new college graduates entering the public relations field were offered an average beginning salary of $21,000. According to a recent salary survey by the Public Relations Journal, public relations managers averaged $44,000.

In the federal government, individuals with a bachelor's degree start at about $23,000; those with a master's degree begin at $28,000. Those in managerial positions average about $46,000. A press secretary's salary will generally fall between $20,000 and $70,000.

RELATED FIELDS

Public relations specialists create and maintain positive attitudes among varying organizations, special interest groups, and the public through effective communication. Other workers who have a similar role include fundraisers, lobbyists, advertising managers, and police officers involved in community relations.

INTERVIEW

Joanne Levine
Public Relations Specialist

Joanne Levine heads her own public relations company, Lekas & Levine Public Relations, Inc.

What the Job's Really Like

"My company specializes in pursuing media publicity for small and mid-sized businesses. Media public relations is probably the most popular among clients, but also the most stressful for the practitioner. Although I also write copy for brochures and business letters and plan some special events, 80 percent of my time is spent trying to help my clients make the news. That is, helping them to appear in newspapers, magazines, and trade publications, and on radio and television. My clients recognize that media publicity is a valuable tool to increase visibility of their products or services, while enhancing their images in the eyes of potential customers, suppliers, business associates, and peers. While paid advertising 'looks like an ad,' editorial appearances add credibility and help to establish the client as an authority in his or her respective field. Whether a fledgling entrepreneur or an established pillar of the business community, there are few people who wouldn't relish the opportunity to make a favorable impression in the news.

"On the other hand, my specialty is probably the least favorite among public relations practitioners. With an ad, you know what day it will appear, what size it will be, and exactly what it will say. With an article, I hold my breath until the client and I read it in the publication. With a taped interview on radio or television, I wait to see if anything was cut or taken out of context. While my press release and phone conversation with an editor might have been chock full of the kind of information I hope they will relay to the public, there are no guarantees such as those in advertising. I work with editors and writers who are always on deadline, always overworked, but nevertheless, always looking for a good angle. For these reasons, my job can be stressful and sometimes plagued with problems that are completely out of my control.

"But when all goes well, there's nothing like it. I have seen the positive results of good, steady media campaigns time and time again. And more than once in a while, a really big media appearance can make an overnight difference in someone's business. The client is on Cloud Nine, his or her phones begin to ring off the hook with new business, and I am showered with praise and gratitude. I often get to know my clients well and enjoy friendly, upbeat working relationships with them. The knowledge that I am helping to make a client's business grow is very rewarding."

How Joanne Levine Got Started

"Although a degree in journalism or communications is certainly desirable, in my particular case, I landed in this career without any planning. Even though I majored in English in college, I didn't really have any ambition to focus on public relations. When my children were babies, I didn't work outside the home but joined various local community groups, such as Friends of the Parks, the PTA, and a Human Relations group. In the course of setting up a fundraiser for one of the organizations, I was paired with a real life PR pro on the publicity committee. She really gave me an education and I became fascinated with her skills. At the same time, my very creative brother was writing music, forming bands, and starting wacky side businesses. One of his companies created and marketed original adult board games he designed. To test my new found skills, each time he introduced a game, I sent out press releases to the media. The first game, Danger Island, even included me as one of the characters. When the reporters came out, I became part of their story. We got spectacular local and national coverage.

"That first project really whet my appetite. From there, I began publicizing my husband's retail stores, more civic groups, and the like. One day, I thought about the fact that I was doing a great job and not getting paid for it. I recruited my brother's wife to help me and we wrote a press release about two sisters-in-law starting a public relations company devoted to small businesses. We got an immediate response from the local chain of newspapers. They wrote a feature article about our company, even though we had no clients. The rest, they say, is history. From that initial article, the phone began to ring and within a month or two, we had five clients. It's been word of mouth ever since.

"My sister-in-law stayed aboard for nine years and finally decided to go back to her first love, teaching. She always felt that even if she did a great job pitching an idea to an editor, it was always that editor who determined how well we did our job. We were always caught in the middle: if the article was great, the client thought we were, too. If the article was small, all the effort we put into the project seemed insignificant. The stress finally got to her and she left. I, on the other hand, thrive on the highs and lows. Not knowing what the day will bring seems exciting to me. One 'yes' from an editor and I'm as happy as a clam."

Expert Advice

"If you want a career in media publicity, I would advise you to read, read, read. Study the format of the newspapers, watch the twelve, five, six and ten o'clock news. Read every magazine you can get your hands on and note how things are laid out. Reporters have certain 'beats,' and if you can zero in on what they write about, half the battle is won. Familiarizing oneself with the media is a never-ending responsibility. While there are a few good media guides that provide information, this is not a substitute for studying the style of an individual person, section, or publication. Also, as the media faces the same cutbacks and consolidations as any other industry, frequent changes in personnel happen at a rapid pace.

"If you don't want to go through the 'trial and error' process as much as I did, try to get an internship with a PR company. I have used graduate students from the Medill School of Journalism at Northwestern University as freelancers several times. Just remember, to make it in this field, you need a good imagination and the ability to find an 'angle.' I can't tell you how many times a client has said, 'I do a better job than anyone else in town and I truly care about my customers.' That's very nice, but it's *Boring*! Find out why he does a better job. What does she do differently? Is the business owner an interesting person? What are his hobbies? The list goes on. You must be able to pick someone's brain until something newsworthy pops out. Then, you must learn who might be fascinated with your information. So much so, that they want to inform their readers about it or share it with their television audience.

"As I look back over the weeks, months, and years, I feel that the most rewarding part of my effort is the knowledge that I have truly made a difference in my clients' businesses, and, consequently, in their lives. The wide diversity of my clientele makes for a job that never gets boring. And when I look ahead, more than anything else I wonder what my next subject will be."

INTERVIEW
Christopher Ryan
Media Planner

Christopher Ryan is a media planner (press secretary) for United States Senator Paul Simon of Illinois. He has worked with the senator for the past eight years.

What's the Job Really Like

"Another individual and myself serve as public spokespeople–liaisons between the media and Senator Simon. The purpose of this is to make sure that conflicting information is not disseminated. If a reporter has a question about what's going on in Congress, we serve as a resource for the answers, whether Senator Simon has a vested interest in the story or not. We pride ourselves on being banks of information on all relevant issues and strive to answer all questions in a prompt and efficient manner.

"We have a very aggressive approach to both the broadcast and print medias–with a heavy emphasis on weekly newspapers. This is the case for two reasons: first, newspapers are well read, and secondly, Senator Simon is himself a former weekly newspaper publisher. Since we all have news backgrounds, we understand the infinite deadlines and political pressures.

"Our workload fluctuates slightly, depending upon whether or not Congress is in session. Each day we begin about 8:00 or 8:30 in the morning and work until about 7:00 at night. On Tuesdays, Wednesdays, and Thursdays we always work later, because that's when the Senate is in session.

"On Monday mornings we usually look at the legislative schedule to find out what topics will be presented on the floor. Then we analyze which ones the state of Illinois has a vested interest in.

"We also need to consider our committee assignments. Senator Simon serves on the Judiciary, the Human Resources and Labor, and the Budget committees. So we must cover those hearings and anticipate the questions we'll have to field. We prepare ourselves to handle everything that's in the news anywhere in the world.

"The best part of this kind of work is making news. It's very gratifying to identify an event or an element of political history that you helped disseminate. The ultimate test of a good press secretary is one who interprets news events as others report it.

"The worst part is fending off disaster. It takes a lot out of you. It's like being a firefighter. Also the work load is very unnerving. You must always be available. People call us at night, on weekends, holidays. It's a grueling pace. You are considered a public servant and are expected to be available–no matter what time it is.

"Ultimately, everything we do reflects upon Senator Simon. Collectively we are him. So our attitudes and our actions are very important. He has devoted himself to his position since coming to the Senate in 1984, and it is my responsibility to let his constituents know what a good job he is doing."

How Christopher Ryan Got Started

"When I went to the University of Illinois and worked at the *Peoria Journal Star*, wire copy was received via teletype machines. As a copy boy, I'd take the copy off the wire and run it to whatever desk was appropriate–sports, state, local desk, whatever. Then I obtained a position as a writer for the *News Gazette* and subsequently worked at Channel 3-WCIA, a CBS affiliate. I remained there while in graduate school, where I received a Masters of Fine Arts degree. (Believe me, I was going to become a movie producer, I majored in media arts with concentrations in the classics, foreign language, social sciences and economics.)

"Senator Simon had read an article I had written and wrote me a letter in response to it. From then on from time to time I would write to him regarding issues or ideas. We kept in touch this way for about four years. When he decided to run for president and began assembling a press staff, I got a call asking if I would be interested in doing press advance for the campaign. Since I wasn't particularly excited about continuing to cover my assigned beat–violent crime–I decided to do just that."

Expert Advice

"To be successful as a press agent, you have to be proactive rather than reactive. The best test of how good you are is how much news you can make. It's important to have good media savvy and an understanding of the way a reporter thinks. You have to work hard, be competitive, and do your job better than your colleagues, because in essence you'll be competing with 99 other senators and 435 members of the House. Ideally, you want one or two stories publicized a day. It's an incredibly competitive environment and if you don't have that fervor you'll get trampled."

INTERVIEW
Marianne Hyatt
Account Executive

Marianne Hyatt is an Account Executive with SJI, Inc., a sales promotion agency in St. Louis, Missouri.

What the Job's Really Like

"I currently work primarily on the Hallmark Cards nationwide account. A typical day consists of any of the following activities: concepting (brainstorming) ideas for client needs; working with the creative department on presentation materials or point-of-purchase designs, talking with potential partners for tie-in promotions (both those that we identify and those who have approached my clients); budget issues (project estimates, profitability review, sourcing, etc.), client meetings (at the office or the clients); project research; reading and routing materials, such as industry periodicals and outside mail; working with our fulfillment company to oversee their work on our projects; and writing copy for various pieces.

"The job encompasses the fun and glamour people think of when they imagine a job in this field. But it also includes frustrating details that no one tells you about. The best part of my job is the people I work with, the experiences I've had (travel, exposure to clients, vast responsibility), and the perks that come along with the job (a great office, wonderful benefits, and a creative atmosphere). The worst part is the long hours and tight deadlines."

How Marianne Hyatt Got Started

"I attended the University of Illinois and received my bachelor's degree in Speech Communication. During college, I held several internships in the public relations field, and felt this was the career I wanted. I worked for a public relations agency (Edelman Worldwide), the promotions/public relations department of my local NBC affiliate, and the public relations department of the chancellor's office of my university. While I didn't get paid for any of these internships (which is standard in this industry), they gave me valuable experience and a 'leg up' when interviewing.

"After college, I attempted to secure an entry-level position at various public relations jobs in St. Louis, but it seemed as if no one would hire someone with 'no practical work experience.' After several months of trying, a friend told me of someone who was an executive for a sales promotion agency. I had never heard of sales promotion, but I gave them a call anyway. After three interviews, they created an entry-level position for me as an account secretary. While ordering office supplies or answering the phone were not my responsibilities, I did assist the account teams with filing, research, sourcing, mailings, and so on. It was an excellent way for me to absorb the work coming out of the agency and get a feel for sales promotion in general and SJI, Inc. more specifically. Within four months I was promoted to account coordinator and have since been promoted to assistant account executive, and most recently, to account executive.

"In my three years at SJI, I have worked on various accounts including Tyson Foods, Porsche Cars North America, Olympus America, Ambassador Cards (a subsidiary of Hallmark), and Hallmark Cards."

Expert Advice

"The first piece of advice I would offer is to gain as much experience as you can through internships. They give you a distinct advantage when interviewing and a headstart once you land your first job.

"Secondly, I would recommend that you research both the career and the company you are most interested in before making any decisions. Look beyond the surface and talk to as many people as you can to get the 'true story' about what to expect.

"Third, don't settle for a job unless you love it. Remember, you'll be spending most of your day there, so if you don't like the environment, the people, or the day-to-day tasks, you won't be happy.

"Finally, merchandise yourself, both during interviews and once you have a job. No one will be aware of your successes (large or small) unless you share them. It's hard to do this without sounding as if you're bragging, but it will bring you additional respect and make you more valuable to the company."

● ● ●

FOR MORE INFORMATION

For current information on careers in public relations, write to:

PR Reporter
P.O. Box 600
Exeter, NH 03833

For information regarding schools, degree programs and other relevant career guidance, contact:

Public Relations Society of America, Inc.
33 Irving Place
New York, NY 10023-2376

For worthwhile career information, approach:

International Association of Business Communications
1 Halladie Plaza, Suite 600
San Francisco, CA 94102

There are several books on advertising that are well worth reading. They include:

Great Jobs for Communications Majors, by Blythe Camenson. NTC Publishing Group, Lincolnwood, Ill.: 1995.
Opportunities in Business Communication Careers, by Robert L. Deen. NTC Publishing Group, Lincolnwood, Ill.: 1987.
Opportunities in Public Relations Careers, by Morris B. Rotman. NTC Publishing Group, Lincolnwood, Ill.: 1988.

CHAPTER 7 Technical Writing

EDUCATION
B.A./B.S. Required

$$$ SALARY/EARNINGS
$20,000 to $30,000 (beginning)
$30,000 to $40,000 (average)
$40,000 to $50,000
        (Senior management)

OVERVIEW

The Society of Technical Communication describes technical communicators as serving as "the bridge between those who create ideas and those who use them." With the wide proliferation of sophisticated products now available to consumers, easy-to-understand instructions are needed to explain how to operate such equipment. These instructions are written by technical writers.

Technical writers prepare assembly instructions, maintenance manuals, parts lists, catalogues, sales promotion materials, and project proposals. Additionally, they write documentation for computer programs, plan and edit technical reports, and create training manuals. Other projects include speeches, articles, presentations, and memos.

A vast number of industries employ technical writers, including chemical, pharmaceutical, aviation, computer, and electronic businesses. Technical writers may also be employed by a research laboratory to write a report on a research topic–anything from to insect invasion to a cure for diabetes. Federal employers include the United States Departments of the Interior, Health and Human Services, Agriculture, the National Aeronautics and Space Administration, and the Department of Defense (which is the largest federal employer). Advertising agencies, newspaper, magazine, and book publishers, professional journals, and colleges and universities also employ technical writers.

Technical writers are also employed by non-scientific members of the community, such as insurance companies who seek to have their industry's terms and procedures explained. Other possible avenues for employment include composing booklets on employee benefits, writing stockholders' reports, and establishing policies and procedures for any type of operation.

THE TECHNICAL WRITING PROCESS

All of the work performed by technical writers represents an attempt to transcribe sophisticated material into more "user-friendly" terms.

The process begins by meeting with all the experts: programmers, engineers, systems analysts, and anyone else who has information to share about the project. Next, the writer performs any relevant independent research. The writer breaks the operation down into small but definite steps or stages, and prepares an outline. A rough draft is written, and then the manuscript is written and rewritten as many times as is necessary. Projects often take weeks or months to complete, which means that a writer may be juggling many projects at one time.

Visual graphics are often used to enhance the reader's understanding, so technical writers must be able to complement the documents they create with tables, diagrams, photos, illustrations, and charts.

TRAINING FOR TECHNICAL WRITERS

Technical writing requires a degree in or some knowledge of a specialized field–business, engineering, or one of the sciences, for example. Many four-year universities and continuing educational institutions offer courses in technical writing. It is possible to major in technical writing at some colleges; others have certificate programs in technical writing, and some offer internships.

In many cases, people with strong writing skills can pick up specialized knowledge on the job. Some technical writers begin as technicians, scientists, or engineers. Others start in technical information departments as editorial or research assistants, develop technical communication skills, and gradually begin technical writing.

Technical writers usually launch their careers in entry-level positions, frequently as assistants to writers who have already established themselves. Assignments typically include updating copy and proofreading. Novices must become familiar with technical jargon and hone their abilities to confer with scientific and technical experts and translate information into simple terms. Research and reporting skills must be sharpened, as well as the ability to write logically, clearly, and precisely.

Although it may be surprising, it is not necessary to be a computer expert to be a technical writer. In one sense, the contrary may be true. If the writer is a beginner, he or she may be able to perceive the information from the point of view of a novice. After all, a technical writer's target audience is made up of novices, and require basic and easy-to-understand explanations.

At some point, technical writers may decide to move from writing to editing, or on to jobs in project leadership, managing documentation, or another specialty.

JOB OUTLOOK

Due to the continuing expansion of scientific and technical information and the ongoing need to disseminate it, the demand for technical writers is expected to increase. Many job openings will also occur as experienced workers transfer to other occupations or leave the labor force. Though there is keen competition in the writing fields, opportunities will be good for technical writers, because only a limited number of writers are able to handle this kind of specialized material.

Many computer companies are concentrated in high-technology centers, such as the Silicon Valley near San Francisco,

California; the Dallas-Fort Worth area of Texas; the Boston area; a research zone in North Carolina; and an area near Philadelphia.

SALARIES FOR TECHNICAL WRITERS

According to a recent *Technical Communicator's Salary Survey,* median annual salaries for technical writers are as follows:

Entry-level – $26,700

Mid-level nonmanagement – $35,000

Mid-level management – $40,000

Senior management – $45,400

Technical writers employed by the federal government earn an average of about $40,000 a year.

RELATED FIELDS

A systematic and logical approach is vital to achieve success as a technical writer. Similar skills are necessary for reporters, public relations specialists, and freelance writers.

INTERVIEW

Chris Santilli
Technical Writer

Originally a full-time company technical writer, Chris Santilli now spends her time as a freelance technical writer.

What the Job's Really Like

"When you're a full-time company technical writer, you're usually working in one industry, so you become an expert in one area. If you're writing for a medical equipment maker, for example, you become an expert on medical equipment. However, you become more of a generalist if you're given a variety of things to write: technical specifications, features, instruction manuals, instructor notes, and so on. As a freelancer, you may also get a variety of assignments–one day you might be writing about software, the next day you might be writing a procedure manual for a store that sells tires.

"As a freelancer or a company employee, you approach projects in pretty much the same way. You begin by meeting with the product expert–most likely a software, manufacturing, mechanical or electrical engineer. Sometimes the product you're dealing with is one that's not on the market yet, sometimes it's not even finished yet. It is likely that this person doesn't speak English as clearly as you do–not that this individual is illiterate by any means, he or she just isn't able to communicate his or her ideas to the lay person. So you have to translate the "engineerese" into more simple language. This means that you have to understand and know how to decipher the lingo. And you must keep in close touch with the expert to be sure that you are saying what he or she intended you to say.

"I work on a project for anywhere from five to six days, up to six or seven weeks. I usually don't have projects that last six months, but many technical writers do. If you're going to write a software manual for Word Perfect, for instance, that's going to take a long time and involve many people. I usually work on projects alone or with one other person, so they normally don't take more than two months.

"Most people hear the phrase 'technical writing' and think of computer manuals. But you could be working for any place that creates any piece of equipment that needs to have something written about it–either how it works, what its specifications are, *anything* that needs documentation or details a procedure.

"When you are fiddling with a product, you sometimes uncover mistakes. Then you go back to the engineer and say, 'Aha, a little something needs to be fixed here.' It's very personally satisfying to find something like that.

"As a freelancer, you spend a lot of time working by yourself. Very seldom do you have contact with marketing people, but occasionally when you do you might feel slightly frustrated with their use of adjectives (they are the bane of the existence of technical writers!).

"There are many pluses to technical writing. The best part is that you work independently making your own schedules and deadlines within the framework of the project specifications. Technical writing is very rewarding because as translator and educator, you are an important, integral member of the team.

"A down side of this work occurs when the product isn't quite ready to be written about. In the software industry, this is sometimes called 'vaporware'–meaning the product doesn't really quite exist, but you must write about it anyway."

How Chris Santilli Got Started

"I earned a bachelor's in Journalism from Northern Illinois University and a master's in Journalism from Syracuse University, but really had no clue what I wanted to do. I worked for nine months at *Stagebill Magazine* as a copy editor and loved it, but they didn't pay much. Then I applied for a job at A.B. Dick as a software writer/editor. That was my first experience with computers. I was placed in front of the computer that I was not only to write *on* but to write *about*. Thank goodness I was given a very well-written software program to use.

"But once I was thrown into this situation I was able to observe others, and I quickly learned by example. I stayed there for about a year and then I moved on. Over the next five years, I kept changing jobs so that I could increase my salary.

"Following this, I spent five years as managing editor at a construction magazine. Then I was laid off, along with many others. I've been freelancing ever since."

Expert Advice

"If you'd like to get an idea about what it's like to be a technical writer, here's some good advice. Choose an activity such as starting your car and sit down and try to explain how to do it in a step-by-step process. Begin the explanation from a point right at your front door. 'Step down the stairs, walk across the patio...'

Remember, nothing can be left out: you *must* mention every detail. A technical writer needs to be obsessed with detail and accuracy.

"I think it also helps to know a touch about statistics and percentages, so that you can make sure that the numbers all add up. You need to have a logical mind in order to understand the logical flow of information and the order of events.

"It's possible to approach this kind of work from a number of different backgrounds–English, history, technical writing. It's advantageous to have a general background in the humanities so that you know how things developed, where you came from, and where you're going. I think as long as you're literate, have a curiosity, think the work is noble, love the English language, and are a persnickety editor, you have a good chance.

"You will also need to be patient, because things don't happen quickly. It may take months to cultivate an assignment, but you have to go though the right paces until the individual in charge of assignments gets in touch with you.

"Always ask for a decent amount of money; never let anyone get away with being cheap. Technical writers generally ask for about $35 an hour. But I don't recommend you work by the hour. I recommend charging by volume of the total project, for example for a procedural manual you might charge $50 for 250 words. Because you're writing technical material, you're going to be writing fewer words than you would with fiction, because you don't have all the adjectives to build up the numbers.

"You really have to find pleasure in this kind of work to be successful at it. Believe it or not, during the summer you'll find me at the beach reading style books just for the fun of it!"

●　　●　　●

FOR MORE INFORMATION

For more information on technical writing, contact:

Society for Technical Communications, Inc.
901 N. Stuart Street, Suite 304
Arlington, VA 22203

There are a number of helpful books on the field, including *The Elements of Technical Writing*, by Gary Blake and Robert W. Bly (Writer's Digest Books, 1993) and *Technical Writing and Communications*, by Jay Gould (VGM Career Horizons, NTC Publishing Group, 1994).

CHAPTER 8 Literary Agents

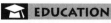 **EDUCATION**
B.A./B.S. Recommended

$$$ SALARY/EARNINGS
$12,000 to $20,000
$20,000 to $30,000

OVERVIEW

All kinds of writers seek out the services of literary agents. Sometimes called "author's representatives," agents serve as the liaisons between authors and the publishers or producers of their work. It is the agent's responsibility to contact editors, submit a writer's manuscripts to them, negotiate contracts and agreements, and in general take the writer's side in dealings with publishers. Of all of these duties, perhaps the most vital is making the connection between the right editor for the right manuscript at the right time. In order to accomplish this, agents need to have hundreds of contacts in the publishing, film, theater, and television industries.

Some agents specialize in particular genres, such as science fiction books or mysteries; others handle only screenplays or computer software. Rarely do agents handle articles, poetry, advertising copy, short stories, or greeting cards.

Today's publishing climate encourages established writers to hire agents. Many publishers will not even deal directly with writers, and will only work with their agents. This is because publishers know that they will be receiving a certain caliber of work from agents and there is no such guarantee from writers. (Though not impossible, it is difficult for non-published writers to find agents to represent them.)

The process begins with an author contacting an agent. This can be done by phone, though more often it is done though a mailed query letter that provides information about a project the writer has completed or is working on. If the agent is interested, he or she will usually request a proposal and a few sample chapters (in the case of non-fiction work) and the whole book (in the case of fiction). Agents should respond to letters, proposals, and manuscripts within three months.

Once an agent agrees to represent an author, both parties enter into an oral or written agreement that specifies the work or works the agent will represent, perhaps the specific period of time he or she will represent the author, and other particulars. Agreements between authors and agents are often subject to termination by either party at any time.

Since agents work strictly on a commission basis, they are only interested in representing writers whose work they can sell. (Whether or not it is fine literature is not necessarily significant.) Usually agents receive a 10 to 15 percent commission of the gross earnings on domestic sales, and perhaps 25 percent on foreign sales. Agents know they'll never sell every manuscript they represent, but they are always looking to take on new and promising clients. Agents will also cease to represent those who no longer seem promising.

Successful agents are conscientious, polite, businesslike, prompt, and accessible to clients and editors. It is important that they are knowledgeable, intuitive, diplomatic, experienced, and successful as salespeople and promoters. They should have exceptional people skills, must keep abreast of trends and happenings in the world of publishing, and be adept at negotiating contracts. A good agent will not give up on a manuscript until it has been given a reasonable chance–perhaps 10 or 15 rejections. Agents also make sure their clients get the correct amount of payment on time and keep them informed of where their manuscripts have been and what the response has been. Some agents provide suggestions for improving potentially sellable manuscripts, as well as general advice for the types of books authors should consider writing based on the trends in the industry.

Agents always negotiate on behalf of the writers they represent, but it is the author who decides whether or not to accept the offer. Agents may offer advice about what they feel is a fair offer, or a great offer, according to what they know about the publishing world at the time. Offers and counter offers are common. If more than one editor is interested, an auction may be held in which two editors bid and the book ultimately goes to the highest bidder.

Once the agent and editor agree to terms, a contract will be sent to the agent. It is his or her job to scrutinize the entire document to make sure the author is protected and receives the best possible terms. All items will be negotiated by the agent and editor. Relevant issues might include advances, royalties, subsidiary rights, out-of-print clauses, warranty, copies printed, paperback distribution, sales to book clubs, advertising, and promotion. Once everything has been ironed out, the agent will send copies of the contract to the author to be signed.

Agents also negotiate serial rights to magazines or newspapers and foreign sales, and may approach other markets, such as television or stage.

A good agent is well-acquainted with the publishing market and stays abreast of new developments and trends. The agent must be sensitive to the needs of his or her clients, and supportive, encouraging, and empathetic.

TRAINING FOR AGENTS

Most agents are former book authors or editors. Those who wish to head their own companies will need a track record with substantial experience and contacts. Those who wish to work for an agenting company may need a college degree, along with credentials as a published author or editor.

JOB OUTLOOK

Only a very small segment of the population can support themselves as agents. Thus competition is very keen and jobs will be scarce. Though anyone can become a self-employed agent, without sufficient clientele the agent cannot stay in business.

SALARIES FOR AGENTS

Salaries for agents will vary widely, from only a few thousand dollars a year to many thousands, depending whether you are self-employed and just establishing your own clientele, or working for an large established agency. Some agents at well-known agencies will take home very respectable salaries, while those building a clientele on their own will struggle.

Larger concentrations of agents and agencies will be found in the New York area, where the publishing world is very prominent. Many television or film agents will be found in the Los Angeles area.

RELATED FIELDS

Similar work is performed by editors, public relations personnel, and advertising specialists.

INTERVIEW

Susan Zeckendorf
Literary Agent

Susan Zeckendorf operates her own company, Susan Zeckendorf

and Associates, Inc.

What the Job's Really Like

"The profession really has two parts: there's a business part and a creative part. Your time is divided between the two.

"In the creative realm, there's the reading, evaluating and sometimes editing of manuscripts. And, of course, an important part of my job is to 'pitch' manuscripts to editors. I don't send anything out without first calling to determine if it's appropriate, and I may find as many as 10 or 12 editors who are interested. (In order to receive that many favorable responses, I will have spent a considerable amount of time on the phone.)

"Once I have determined who I will be sending manuscripts to, I concentrate on creating the persuasive cover letter that must go along with the project.

"On the business side, I might be examining royalty statements of authors and sending out payments. Or I might be checking on subsidiary rights, translation rights, or film or television rights. For all of those subsidiary rights I have sub-agents all over the world. I keep in touch with them to see how they're doing in selling or placing my projects.

"Each day I get about 20 query letters (which means that I'm receiving 3000 or 4000 such letters a year) from potential authors who would like me to take a look at their work. And I must respond to those as quickly as possible. In addition, I must follow up on projects that are already with publishers. Besides all of this, there are an endless number of conversations and lunches with authors and editors. Very often, lunch is a time when I'll pitch books or editors will want to go over my list to see which authors interest them, or I'll meet with authors about their works.

"Though I like to work alone, I enjoy the fact that this is very much a people-oriented business. You're always involved with authors, editors, contract people, and others. Sociability is at the center of this type of work.

"Most aspects of being an agent are enjoyable and up-beat. It's sometimes disheartening, however, to take on a project that you really believe in and see it rejected everywhere. But you have to be able to deal with rejection because that's also part of the job."

How Susan Zeckendorf Got Started

"I graduated from Wellesley and then got a master's in Psychology at Columbia. For a while I worked as a counseling psychologist. My entrance into working as an agent about 15 years ago was really by happenstance. Both my father and my stepfather had books that needed looking after. For one book, I had to get the rights back, the other I wanted to sell into paperback. So I began to learn a little about the business. Then I edited manuscripts for two friends who had written novels. When they expressed a desire to hire an agent, I decided this was something that I would like to do. I learned the ropes from two other friends in the publishing business; one was an agent, the other was an editor. And a publishing attorney taught me what I needed to know about negotiating contracts.

"In the beginning it takes time getting to know the editors. And you have to become familiar not only with the publishing house as a whole, but who is focusing on mysteries, westerns, literary fiction, and so on. I belong to several professional groups and I've met editors that way. Sometimes one editor will refer me to another. Your name gets around and editors tend to get in touch with you. If they don't, you get in touch with them.

"My agency is very small and I usually work with no more than 35 clients at a time. And if I believe in something, I may send it out as many as 25 times. There's nothing more thrilling than working hard on a project, sending it out over and over again, finding a publisher, and finally holding the finished product in your hand."

Expert Advice

"To achieve success as an agent, you need good business sense in order to know what a project is worth. Sales, organization, and negotiation skills are also vital.

"For those who might be considering entering this profession, I would recommend that you work for an agent to learn everything you need to know. This way you'll hopefully be drawing a regular salary as you are learning. Once you are on your own, it takes time to build up a successful business. I also think working in publishing would be valuable, because you would be acquiring much of the information and skills necessary for your career as an agent."

●　●　●

FOR MORE INFORMATION

To learn more about becoming an agent, contact:

Society of Authors' Representatives, Inc.
39 1/2 Washington Square South
New York, NY 10012

You can look up agents in the most recent issue of the *Writer's Market* or *Literary Market Place (LMP)*. Two helpful books are *Literary Agents*, by Michael Larsen (Writer's Digest Books) and *The Indispensable Writer's Guide*, by Scott Edelstein (HarperCollins).

CHAPTER 9 Communications Educators

OVERVIEW

Many people who have a love for language also have a desire to instill this love in others. So they become teachers.

⌂ EDUCATION
B.A./B.S. Required

$$$ SALARY/EARNINGS
$30,000 to $40,000

Teaching at the High School Level

The general area of communications may be taught in high schools or in colleges and universities. At the high-school level, classes may be called English, journalism, or communications. Almost everyone can remember their favorite high school English teacher. Why is this so? Because, if you were lucky, he or she provided you with a strong foundation in writing and the confidence to express yourself. Hopefully, this will be something you will pass along to your own students.

Requirements for high-school teachers vary from state to state, but everyone must earn a bachelor's degree from a college or university that has a state-approved curriculum. This would include a prescribed course of study and classroom experience as a student teacher, usually for a six-month period. If you wish to teach journalism classes, you can choose to major in English or journalism and take education classes, or choose education as your major and take journalism or English classes. Once you have completed your studies, most states require applicants to successfully pass a teacher certification competency examination. These tests are designed to measure subject-matter mastery, basic skills, and teaching capabilities.

Some states allow you to teach with a provisional certification immediately upon obtaining your degree. Regular certification is attained by working with an experienced educator for one or two years while completing the necessary education courses.

When certificates come up for renewal, additional coursework may be required. In some states, a master's degree may be mandatory.

As a teacher at the high-school level, you may be employed by public or private institutions. Private schools are usually less stringent and often don't make state certification a requirement.

It is not unusual for teachers of English, communications, or journalism to be assigned to teach other classes, such as creative writing, social studies, or history.

Secondary schools occasionally hire visiting artists or artists-in-residence who are established authors or poets. These individuals are acknowledged professionals in their field and do not need to have teaching credentials or even a college education.

EDUCATION
Post Graduate Required

$$$ SALARY/EARNINGS
$40,000 to $50,000

Teaching at the College Level

The hierarchy of college educators includes instructors, assistant professors, associate professors, and professors. New faculty members are generally hired as instructors or assistant professors, depending on their background and experience.

An average teaching load is 12 to 16 hours per week, not counting preparation time and staff conferences and meetings. Students are usually required to turn in essays, term papers, and other written work, which educators must evaluate, grade, and return to students. In addition, teachers are expected to be available to advise students about career choices, courses, or other matters. This can translate to three to six additional hours per week (usually slotted as office hours, where teachers make themselves available to students on a regular basis). Staff members may also be called on to aid in special projects, internships, graduate theses, and registration; serve on department and university committees; and develop proposals for research grants. Those who become department heads have additional responsibilities.

In addition to teaching, educators are usually expected to publish written work. Those who are employed at four-year institutions are expected to produce more than those who are on-staff at community colleges; teachers at community colleges are usually assigned a larger number of classes. And professors in the arts may receive credit for published work by writing novels or plays.

Communications curriculum and departments may be set up a variety of ways. English departments may offer creative writing, composition, and technical writing courses. Communications and journalism might be divided into two separate departments. Public relations and advertising may be housed under a variety of headings or one of their own. Some smaller schools can offer only a handful of classes; they might be listed under theater, speech, or English.

Writers who teach and teachers who write usually agree that the teaching keeps them alert and proficient writers.

TRAINING FOR COMMUNICATIONS EDUCATORS

Most college and university faculty are in four academic ranks: professor, associate professor, assistant professor, and instructor. A few are considered lecturers. Most are hired as instructors or assistant professors.

Teaching at the college level requires a minimum of a master's degree. Large numbers of doctorate-level instructors will be found at four-year institutions. (Doctoral programs usually take four to seven years of full-time study beyond the bachelor's level to complete.) At four-year universities, associate professors have a minimum of three years of university level teaching experience along with a doctorate degree.

A major step in the traditional academic career is being given tenure. Newly hired faculty serve a specific period (usually seven years) under year-to-year contracts. Their record of teaching, research, and overall contribution to the institution is then reviewed, and tenure is granted if the review is favorable and positions are available. Once an educator receives tenure, he or she is guaranteed a position on the faculty for life, unless there is a serious breach on his or her part.

JOB OUTLOOK

Employment of secondary school teachers is expected to increase faster than the average for all occupations through the year 2005. Employment of college and university faculty is expected to increase about as fast as the average for all occupations through the same period, as enrollments in higher education increase. Other additional openings will become available as older faculty members retire. Faculty retirements are expected to increase significantly from the late 1990s through 2005, as a significant number of faculty members who entered the profession during the 1950s and 1960s reach retirement age.

SALARIES FOR COMMUNICATIONS EDUCATORS

Salaries vary according to faculty rank and type of institution. In general, educators at four-year institutions earn more than those who teach at two-year schools and community colleges. According to a survey by the American Association of University Professors, salaries for full-time faculty average $46,300 (for nine-month contracts): professors earn an average of $59,500; associate professors, $44,100; assistant professors, $36,800; and instructors, $27,700. Many faculty members earn additional income through consulting, teaching extra courses, conducting research, or writing for publication during the summer months.

RELATED FIELDS

College and university faculty function both as teachers and researchers who communicate information and ideas. Related occupations include elementary and secondary school teachers, librarians, writers, consultants, lobbyists, trainers and employee development specialists, and policy analysts. Faculty research activities are frequently similar to those of project managers and scientists.

INTERVIEW
Steve Falcone
Associate Professor of English

Steve Falcone is Associate Professor of English at John A. Logan College in Southern Illinois.

What the Job's Really Like

"The community college is an exciting place to be. We have a wide range of people and that keeps things interesting and fulfilling all the time. I am a writing teacher: my job is to cover the basic composition sequence. We also offer literature courses, and I teach a lot of essay writing. I am in charge of a creative writing course, which I developed over the years myself, so of course it's my favorite. I teach other things, too, such as mythology.

"Basically, it comes down to the fact that I have about 200 students who write about five or six essays in a semester and about 100 who write a research paper. My job is to clean up their writing, make sense of it, give them structure, and help them develop their ideas. I usually teach six classes a week; I bunch them together on certain days so that I can write on my days off. I also see students in my office, and I am the editor of the student magazine.

"At the end of the day I'm usually in the theater, directing a play, being in one, or writing one.

"I help a wide range of students—from those who are just out of high school to those a generation older who are returning students. My students' youth and enthusiasm is tremendous. It keeps me young and I like that. I am a firm believer that attitude is everything—if you go in with a positive perspective, you'll make great gains. I enjoy watching people overcome their initial fears and inhibitions and find out that they have skills and talent."

How Steve Falcone Got Started

"I received a bachelor's degree from LaSalle College, a liberal arts college in the east, before coming to the midwest to earn a master's degree in English from Southern Illinois University. Following that, I completed quite a bit of PhD coursework, but I stopped somewhere short of a degree. Then I traveled around for a while, to Ireland, England, and, back in the United States, to Texas.

"I've been teaching for the past 12 years; 10 of which have been at Logan. Theater is something I've been enjoying since its inception here at the beginning of my teaching days on this campus.

"It's a joy to be working here. The average length of staff members' experience is probably about 13 years. Everyone here is committed to hard work and serving our pupils. We focus only on teaching students: we don't have to publish anything. This is not to say that some teachers have not done so, only that we are not required to do so. We are involved in other interesting projects as well, such as a teacher-exchange program in England from which I just returned after spending two weeks teaching drama."

Expert Advice

"The first bit of advice I would offer is to tell you that you may have to put in substantial effort and need some luck in finding a job. They're not easy to come by. When Logan was founded, they were content to hire educators with master's degrees. Now they're looking for those with PhDs. But I still think you can help yourself by making a choice early on. Decide if you like the idea of working exclusively with students or if you wish to combine your efforts with research. I have a problem with the universities caught in the middle of that, because sometimes students end up with teachers who don't want to teach classes. Figure out where your love lies. If you want to be a teacher, figure out the best way to get into the classroom. I have colleagues at the university who find it difficult to believe the number of classes I teach and the number of papers I evaluate, but that's OK. I like dealing with people on paper. Decide if you love language and enjoy breaking it down and getting it back on track for people.

"Bringing a positive attitude to the work place does wonders. You should understand that you have a lot of power as a teacher. And I vote for enthusiasm and levity, rather than criticism and intimidation. The classroom should be a friendly, nurturing environment. When it is, people come in droves, and they will be happier and grow faster."

•   •   •

FOR MORE INFORMATION

To learn more about teaching communications, contact:

American Association of University Professors
1012 14th Street, N.W.
Washington, DC 20005

National Education Association
1201 16th Street N.W.
Washington, DC 20036

For information on unionized activities contact:

American Federation of Teachers
555 New Jersey Avenue, N.W.
Washington, DC 20001

Obtain a copy of *Opportunities in Teaching*, by Janet Fine (NTC Publishing Group, 1995), and *Careers in Education*, by Roy Edelfelt, Ed.D (NTC Publishing Group, 1995).

CHAPTER 10 Other Communications Careers

OVERVIEW

The world of communications careers is enormous, and though opportunities in some fields can be limited, ultimately there are any number of communications careers you might follow. These include freelance writing, multimedia, playwriting, screenwriting, song writing, book reviewing, ghostwriting, and grant writing. And don't forget speech writing, comedy writing, and poetry writing!

EDUCATION
B.A./B.S. Recommended

$$$ SALARY/EARNINGS
Minimum wage to $12,000
$12,000 to $20,000

Freelance Writing

Many people who love to write become freelance writers. They are self-employed individuals who may accept projects from one or a number of clients. Some freelancers specialize and write in only one area, such as educational writing; others perform a variety of writing tasks.

Freelancers enjoy many privileges; they may focus on assignments that interest them, set their own hours, work from home (or anywhere for that matter), wear whatever is comfortable, choose their clients, and take vacations whenever they wish. On the flip side are negative factors, such as an erratic cash flow, a scarcity of work, isolation, and an overwhelming number of roles you must fulfill, such as marketer, publicist, author, and bill collector.

One should not consider doing this kind of work full-time until a clientele base has been established. Stories of overnight success are fictional. Writers put in a tremendous amount of hours, energy, and effort over a period of months and years in order to make freelance writing a full-time career option.

Freelancers often begin their careers by writing in an area that they are familiar with: for instance, a boat enthusiast would do well to write about what to look for when purchasing a new boat.

Where do freelancers get their assignments? They are offered assignments by newspapers, magazines, public relations concerns, any and all types of businesses, non-profit organizations, educational concerns, and publishers. The list goes on and on. The exact nature of the work will vary from feature articles to columns, newsletters, brochures, sales letters, or book reviews.

A career in freelance writing requires a large measure of self-discipline. After all, there is no one around you telling you to get to work. You have to know (and keep remembering) that intrinsically. You must have a strong goal orientation, along with the ability to pay attention to detail and an understanding that you must *never* miss a deadline.

Though freelance writers work alone most of the time, they need to have strong people skills, both to ingratiate themselves to editors, project leaders, and publishers, and to work together with others on writing assignments. The ability to be persuasive over the phone and a good personal presence are especially important.

Organizational skills are also important, as freelancers must juggle a number of projects at the same time. A typical week may involve developing an outline for an article, composing a sales letter, conducting 10 interviews, and going to the library to conduct research.

It's important to keep careful records of where all of your query letters, poems, and manuscripts are; the status of new markets you are trying to break into; and all financial transactions.

Since freelance writers are self-employed, bear in mind that they receive no fringe benefits and must arrange their own medical insurance.

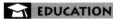 **EDUCATION**
B.A./B.S. Required

$$$ SALARY/EARNINGS
$20,000 to $30,000

Multimedia

The term "multimedia" can be used to mean several things. It can refer to a CD-ROM program, a slide presentation, an audiovisual workshop, or a succession of charts and graphs along with photography or video. Positions in this field may be found in business and industry, in religious organizations, in advertising and public relations concerns, and in all levels of government. It is possible to become an audiovisual producer, an audiovisual writer, a production assistant, or an audiovisual manager.

EDUCATION
B.A./B.S. Recommended

$$$ SALARY/EARNINGS
Minimum wage to $12,000
$12,000 to $20,000

Playwriting, Screenwriting, and Song Writing

Playwrights are responsible for creating the scripts for stage plays seen in radio and television productions, Broadway and off-Broadway theaters, community theaters, and university theater productions. They must be able to bring action, dialogue, and visual dynamics to their scripts.

Screenwriters write the scripts for television or films. Usually they work for motion picture studios.

Songwriters might be responsible for lyrics or musical scores or both. Sometimes lyricists and composers work together to create a harmonious duo, such as Rogers and Hammerstein.

Book Reviewers

Some book reviewers work as freelancers; others are employed by newspapers, magazines, television stations, or radio stations. They evaluate new books according to the works' literary quality and mass appeal. Reviews should point out the strengths and weaknesses of the book and why the reviewer formed a particular opinion of the book. Very few individuals work as full-time book reviewers; often they are book authors also.

Ghostwriters

Ghostwriters may be the *real* authors of anything from an article to a short story to an entire book. The writers generally do not get credit for doing the work; it appears as if someone else did the work – after all, *their* name goes on the cover. Famous people often hire ghostwriters to write their autobiographies.

Grant Writers

Grant writers must have strong communication skills, in addition to a sound background in fundraising. They are usually employed by non-profit organizations, for whom they research, cultivate, and negotiate all data relative to grants. Without them, many organizations would cease to exist.

TRAINING FOR OTHER COMMUNICATIONS CAREERS

College degrees are usually not necessary for freelance writing, playwriting, screenwriting, songwriting, book reviewing, and ghostwriting. However, most successful writers these days do have degrees or some form of formal training. A sufficient background in writing is, of course, imperative, along with strong oral and written presentation skills. It is important to build a list of credits that will add substance to your rèsumè.

A four-year degree is necessary to obtain a career in multimedia. Employers usually prefer a major in communications, but may consider related degrees such as journalism.

JOB OUTLOOK

Competition for freelance work is fierce, especially for those who are not established writers. However, in times of downsizing, companies often turn to greater numbers of freelancers in order to fill the voids left by laying off full-time employees.

Competition is extremely keen for the writers involved in playwriting, screenwriting, and songwriting–ultimately, it all depends on inspiration and luck.

SALARIES FOR OTHER COMMUNICATIONS CAREERS

Earnings for freelancers vary widely. Part-time and beginners may earn as little as $1,000 per year or less, but successful part-timers may earn between $5,000 and $15,000. Some magazines pay nothing for articles; others pay $1.00 per word (or more). Experienced writers may receive $600 to $4,000 per article. Writers who obtain book contracts usually receive advances against future royalties. The amount that authors make from books will depend upon the royalty rate and how many books are sold, but only best-selling authors like Tom Clancy and Danielle Steel receive a *lot* of money from their books.

RELATED FIELDS

All of the careers in this chapter require the ability to write effectively. Other such careers include marketing and advertising professionals; newspaper, book, or magazine publishing personnel; and public relations employees.

INTERVIEW

Liz Ball
Garden Communicator

Liz Ball is a garden communicator and co-owner of New Response, Incorporated.

What the Job's Really Like

"In 1991 my associate and I came out with a book called *Yardening*, and we are now putting the finishing touches on a new book called *Lawn Care for Yardeners*. Having given many talks over the years, we have come to the conclusion that there is a world of people out there who have custody of plants but are not gardeners and don't want to be. We call them 'yardeners,' people who want to take care of their property, have it look nice, and then go and play golf. We decided that these are the people who need help, and so these are the people who we have made our market.

"In an effort to reach this audience, we've done a number of things. One is the newspaper column I write for four regional newspapers. It's designed for home owners and it's called–you guessed it–'yardening.' I find this to be very challenging work. The column consists of five topics that I feature each session. In the process of writing the column, I do a considerable amount of responding to mail, which I really enjoy. In addition, I'm always scanning newspapers and magazines for potential topics I can use. But I am responsible for the concept of the column and the way I compose it.

"In another effort to reach homeowners, our company publishes what we call 'yard care tip sheets.' We produce them on desktop publishing. Over the years, we've put together an inventory of almost 200 tip sheets. And, when necessary, I have the responsibility of revising them.

"I also work on preparing the speeches that I give as an outreach effort to get information to homeowners. I've appeared before garden clubs, neighborhood associations, and other groups. I feel that people need to be knowledgeable, even if they are not performing the work themselves. For example, they need to be able to tell the gardener to mow the lawn no shorter than two inches.

"We also mount an educational display called 'Yardening Academy.' We bring it to home and garden shows offered by large cities. Plans have already been made for nine cities in the upcoming future. My partner Jeff has the primary responsibility for this, but I will be flying in to certain cities to help."

How Liz Ball Got Started

"After receiving a bachelor's degree in teaching English at the secondary level from the University of Rochester, I attended Brown University where I earned a master's degree in History. For many years after that, I taught English and social studies. I was assigned to a number of differing situations, but two were particularly noteworthy and rewarding. One job was teaching returning Vietnam War veterans on disability who had never finished high school. Another rewarding experience was returning to the area where I grew up and teaching at the high school I had attended as a teen.

"My career as a gardening writer began when my husband and I moved to a home that had a vegetable garden. Finding ourselves in an area with enthusiastic organic gardeners, we became interested in caring for our vegetable garden. We soon realized that there wasn't a good book available for beginners. To answer all our questions, we had to consult four or five sources. So my husband decided to write a book that would fill this void. He wrote a proposal and sent it to several publishers. One publisher said they were doing something along the same lines but asked if he would be interested in doing something else. That was our entrance into the world of garden communications.

"We turned our yard into a research area and gradually I got more and more involved. Eventually I performed all the editing and rewriting. Then, when we needed slides for speeches, I began to take pictures. Together we published six books for Rodale Press. And even though we are no longer married, we still collaborate and run the business together."

Expert Advice

"I would stress the importance of being computer literate. There's so much value in making use of computer technology. For instance, we have a database program that has a catalogue of my slides.

"It's also advantageous to know how desktop publishing works. This helps you conceptualize what you are doing and gives you some idea of how your project should be packaged.

"Investigate the possibilities of joining a professional organization and find one that is right for you. The Garden Writers Association of America has been invaluable to us and it has provided us with a wealth of contacts. When you are a freelancer, you really need the support of others who are engaged in the same kind of work. Phone and fax contact become extremely important.

"If you're going to write, you need to be familiar with outlets for your writing. We receive almost every major and a large number of minor gardening publications–a total of 20 to 30.

Obtain the magazine's editorial guidelines before you submit anything, so that you can follow their directions and write to specifically named contacts. Follow up with a query letter. I would advise you not to complete an article before getting at least an 'on speculation' approval from an editor. (This means there is interest but no promise to buy if the finished piece does not meet his or her specifications.)

"I know a number of individuals who have salaried positions as editors of magazines or newspapers, or who write for public relations firms. Working on a freelance basis full-time is entirely different. Just because you can write does not mean you have an MBA in marketing and sales–and you *must* be able to perform these duties also, or find someone who can do them for you. You have to be able to cultivate and juggle a lot of things that are happening all at once. I always keep lots of irons in the fire and constantly check to see if any heat up. Invariably one does, and then it's time to concentrate on pursuing that iron until hopefully another one heats up.

"Remember: the best way of becoming a good writer is to be an outstanding reader. Do as much as you can in as many areas as possible. I guarantee it *will* pay off."

INTERVIEW

Mary Nelson
Grant Writer

Mary Nelson is a grant writer for a non-profit organization in a large city.

What the Job's Really Like

"My typical day includes writing or updating a draft or final copy of a grant or grant report. If I'm not writing something related to a grant, I'm meeting or talking on the phone with someone and developing a grant or a grant report. I meet with 'program people' (the individuals who actually carry out the projects) to discuss the specifics of projects for which we are seeking funding or have received funding. Basically, I'm always updating my calendar of report and grant timetables and deadlines and always reworking grants and reports.

"I usually go to the library one to three times a week to conduct donor/prospect research. This means that I try to determine which companies, foundations, and individuals are most likely to give money to our organization, based on such characteristics as previous donation patterns to other organizations. I perform in-depth research on groups who are already our donors. With this information, I may prepare one or more call/visit reports per day for use by a board member, volunteer, staff, or chief officer during a solicitation or cultivation activity. I also analyze the giving history of donors to determine who requires additional research and who are prospective major donors.

"The individual activities of my job are interesting and fun. However, bureaucracy within the non-profits I work and have worked for is sometimes irritating. Many times people are resistant to change; this often prohibits me from doing my job completely. Additionally, non-profits are notorious for overworking their staff without compensating them with time away from the office or money remuneration. I am often expected to work long hours by management.

"I'm not sure if it is true for all fundraising offices, but through my own experience and that of my colleagues, there seems to be a relatively high turnover rate in this profession. Part of this might be related to the pressure of having to raise large amounts of money to support much-needed programming for the population your organization serves. It is disheartening to know that, if you do not reach your fundraising goal, needed programs or staff may be cut. Non-profits seem to tend to rely too heavily on their fundraising departments.

"Additionally, fundraising managers, in my experience, do not necessarily have solid managerial experience (my last two managers had little or no prior management experience). Probably as a direct result of this lack of experience, the departments I have worked for have not been well-managed."

How Mary Nelson Got Started

"I began to develop fundraising skills when I was a telemarketer in high school and college. At the time I didn't even realize that this was an actual field of employment. When I was in college, I was also a Panhellenic (sorority) Council officer; part of my responsibilities included organizing and publicizing Panhellenic-sponsored events. This was my 'introduction to event planning.' I worked part-time at the University of Illinois Foundation, tele-marketing alums for donations to the university.

"Then I joined the United States Peace Corps after graduation. In the Peace Corps, I was taught by my Associate Peace Corps Director how to write grants in a five-day training workshop sponsored by the U.S. Agency for International Development (A.I.D.). I utilized these skills to write grants to fund projects in my village, as well as to teach others in my village how to write grants. Up until the end of my Peace Corps experience, I never thought of entering the field of grant writing, even though I had established some good, generalist fundraising experience and skills.

"When my Peace Corps term ended abruptly, one year early due to illness, I was thrown into a quick job search because I had missed all of the graduate school application deadlines. And I couldn't enter either of my fields of interest (political science and psychology) without an advanced degree. So I made the decision to work for a non-profit agency. I applied for jobs in counseling, administration, and development. All of the related work and volunteer experience I had helped me to get an entry-level job that focused mainly on grant writing.

"My generalist experience with emphasis on the grant writing and donor/prospect research helped me move into a mid-level, more specialized job at another non-profit agency."

Expert Advice

"Grant writing generally requires the following skills for an entry-level position: excellent oral, written and interpersonal skills, accomplishments in planning and organizing; flexibility; and in general, a bachelor's degree. Many times, these entry-level jobs are relatively low paying (high teens to mid-twenties).

"If you have been in the work force for more than one to three years, your work experience in another area of expertise may enable you to obtain a mid-, advanced-, or management-level position in an organization. For instance, if you work as a nurse at a hospital and are interested in applying for a mid-level job in your hospital's development office, your background with the hospital–coupled with some volunteer fundraising experience–may be the fit that an employer is looking for, rather than someone who might have a solid fundraising background but no knowledge of health care issues. Additionally, if you have a great background in sales or corporate event planning, these skills may transfer to the non-profit arena. It is important to look at the rudimentary skills that you've developed throughout your work and volunteer experience.

"When looking for fundraising jobs, check fundraising publications, such as *The Chronicle of Philanthropy*; fundraising professional associations, like the National Society for Fund Raising Executives (NSFRE); the local Foundation Center Library (which may have NSFRE job listings); and local newspapers."

● ● ●

FOR MORE INFORMATION

To learn more about communications careers or opportunities for freelancers, consult *Writer's Market*, *The Writer's Handbook*, or *Literary Market Place*. For further information write to:

Author's League of America
330 West 42nd Street, 29th Floor
New York, NY 10036

American Society of Journalists and Authors
1501 Broadway, Suite 302
New York, NY 10036

Women in Communications
2101 Wilson Blvd., Suite 417
Arlington, VA 22201

VGM CAREER BOOKS

BUSINESS PORTRAITS
Boeing
Coca-Cola
Ford
McDonald's

CAREER DIRECTORIES
Careers Encyclopedia
Dictionary of Occupational Titles
Occupational Outlook Handbook

CAREERS FOR
Animal Lovers; Bookworms; Caring
People; Computer Buffs; Crafty
People; Culture Lovers;
Environmental Types; Fashion Plates;
Film Buffs; Foreign Language
Aficionados; Good Samaritans;
Gourmets; Health Nuts; History
Buffs; Kids at Heart; Music Lovers;
Mystery Buffs; Nature Lovers; Night
Owls; Number Crunchers; Plant
Lovers; Shutterbugs; Sports Nuts;
Travel Buffs; Writers

CAREERS IN
Accounting; Advertising; Business;
Child Care; Communications;
Computers; Education; Engineering;
the Environment; Finance;
Government; Health Care; High
Tech; Horticulture & Botany;
International Business; Journalism;
Law; Marketing; Medicine; Science;
Social & Rehabilitation Services

CAREER PLANNING
Beating Job Burnout
Beginning Entrepreneur
Big Book of Jobs
Career Planning & Development for
    College Students &
    Recent Graduates
Career Change
Career Success for People with
    Physical Disabilities
Careers Checklists
College and Career Success for Students
    with Learning Disabilities
Complete Guide to Career Etiquette
Cover Letters They Don't Forget
Dr. Job's Complete Career Guide
Executive Job Search Strategies
Guide to Basic Cover Letter Writing
Guide to Basic Résumé Writing
Guide to Internet Job Searching
Guide to Temporary Employment
Job Interviewing for College Students
Joyce Lain Kennedy's Career Book

Out of Uniform
Parent's Crash Course in Career
    Planning
Slame Dunk Résumés
Up Your Grades: Proven Strategies
    for Academic Success

CAREER PORTRAITS
Animals; Cars; Computers;
Electronics; Fashion; Firefighting;
Music; Nature; Nursing; Science;
Sports; Teaching; Travel; Writing

GREAT JOBS FOR
Business Majors
Communications Majors
Engineering Majors
English Majors
Foreign Language Majors
History Majors
Psychology Majors
Sociology Majors

HOW TO
Apply to American Colleges and
    Universities
Approach an Advertising Agency and
    Walk Away with the Job You Want
Be a Super Sitter
Bounce Back Quickly After
    Losing Your Job
Change Your Career
Choose the Right Career
Cómo escribir un currículum vitae en
    inglés que tenga éxito
Find Your New Career Upon
    Retirement
Get & Keep Your First Job
Get Hired Today
Get into the Right Business School
Get into the Right Law School
Get into the Right Medical School
Get People to Do Things Your Way
Have a Winning Job Interview
Hit the Ground Running in Your
    New Job
Hold It All Together When You've
    Lost Your Job
Improve Your Study Skills
Jumpstart a Stalled Career
Land a Better Job
Launch Your Career in TV News
Make the Right Career Moves
Market Your College Degree
Move from College into a
    Secure Job
Negotiate the Raise You Deserve
Prepare Your Curriculum Vitae

Prepare for College
Run Your Own Home Business
Succeed in Advertising When all You
Succeed in College
Succeed in High School
Take Charge of Your Child's Early
    Education
Write a Winning Résumé
Write Successful Cover Letters
Write Term Papers & Reports
Write Your College Application Essay

MADE EASY
College Applications
Cover Letters
Getting a Raise
Job Hunting
Job Interviews
Résumés

**ON THE JOB: REAL PEOPLE
    WORKING IN...**
Communications
Health Care
Sales & Marketing
Service Businesses

OPPORTUNITIES IN
This extensive series provides detailed
    information on more than 150
    individual career fields.

RÉSUMÉS FOR
Advertising Careers
Architecture and Related Careers
Banking and Financial Careers
Business Management Careers
College Students &
    Recent Graduates
Communications Careers
Computer Careers
Education Careers
Engineering Careers
Environmental Careers
Ex-Military Personnel
50+ Job Hunters
Government Careers
Health and Medical Careers
High School Graduates
High Tech Careers
Law Careers
Midcareer Job Changes
Nursing Careers
Re-Entering the Job Market
Sales and Marketing Careers
Scientific and Technical Careers
Social Service Careers
The First-Time Job Hunter

 VGM Career Horizons
a division of *NTC Publishing Group*
4255 West Touhy Avenue
Lincolnwood, Illinois 60646–1975